INTERVIEW QUESTIONS FOR JOB

How to Answer, Best Skills, Self-Control, Phone Interview, Job Interview, Mindset Technique

Volume 1

MAX GORDON

Copyright © 2020 Max Gordon

INTERVIEW QUESTIONS FOR JOB

TABLE OF CONTENTS

INTERVIEW QUESTIONS FOR JOB

INTRODUCTION

The clue to a successful job interview is preparation. If an interviewee is not prepared for an interview, the result can only be 50% successful. Today's employees can do two types of interviews; it may be a telephone interview or a personal interview. Preparation for both interviews is essential because you can never know what kind of interview your employer will do. So what are the types of preparations you need to make for telephone or personal interviews?

There are three categories in preparation for an interview; these are physical preparation, mental preparation, and psychological preparation. In personal interviews, you must prepare for the three categories, while in telephone interviews; it is enough to worry about mental and psychological preparation.

Therefore, personal interviewing requires more preparation. In physical preparation, you should remember that good health and careful care increase your confidence and radiate positive energy into you. This will grant you an edge over all other candidates. The researchers wanted to see an energetic, healthy, and positive job instead of a sick and negative job. Also, your physical appearance will make the first impression on the interview panel, so your physical preparation is of the utmost importance.

Sit down in the interview panel and think about how a respondent will dress as you walk into the park. Or does he look as though he has a date? In the art of war, to win, you have to think like your opponent. It's the same in interviews, you have to think like the interviewer. If you were them, how did you like the interviewee? What would you like to see during the interview?

However, in telephone interviews, physical appearance is not important because the interviewer will not see you during the interview. So, no matter if you're inside, you're in pajamas.

Mental preparation is important for personal and telephone interviews, as this will be the deciding factor in whether or not the panel will employ you. Mental preparation is sometimes called intellectual preparation. This will measure your job qualifications, how well you know the job description if you are mentally equipped to do the job.

These are just many of the things you need to think about when preparing for job interviews.

WHAT IS JOB INTERVIEW

A job interview is an interview that consists of a conversation between a job applicant and an employer representative that is conducted to assess whether the candidate should be insured. Interviews are one of the popularly used devices for employee selection. Interviews vary in the degree of structure of the questions, from a completely unstructured and free communication to a structured interview in which the candidate is asked a predetermined list of questions in a specific order; structured interviewing is generally a more accurate predictor of which candidates will be most suitable, according to research studies.

A job interview usually precedes the hiring choice. The interview is usually preceded by an assessment of the curricula submitted by interested candidates, possibly examining the questions, or reading numerous resumes. Then, after this list, a small number of interview candidates are selected.

Job interview opportunities also involve networking events and job fairs. The job interview is viewed as one of the most valuable tools for evaluating potential employees. It also requires significant resources from employers but has been shown to be remarkably reliable in identifying the right person for the job. An interview also allows the applicant to assess the corporate culture and employment needs.

Different series of job interviews and/or other candidate selection methods can be used when there are several candidates or when the job is particularly difficult or desirable. Previous cycles, sometimes referred to as "selection interviews", may involve fewer employer employees and, in general, will be much shorter and less profound. Phone maintenance is becoming more and more common. This is particularly common when the requirements are not close to the employer and have the benefit of keeping costs low for both parties. Since 2003, the interview has been conducted through video conferencing software, such as skype. Usually, after all, candidates have been interviewed, the employer selects the candidates most wanted and starts negotiating a job offer.

TYPES OF INTERVIEW

There are some types of interviews that companies can conduct. However, the same for all types of interviews is the idea of the interview structure. The degree of structuring, development, and conduct of an interview in the same way for all candidates depends on the number of certain elements included in that interview. In general, the interview can be standardized both in terms of content (ie, what are the questions) and in the assessment process (ie, how are the answers? Candidates for the questions are noted). When an interview is regulated, it increases the likelihood that an interviewee's notes are due to the quality of their answers rather than factors that are not as important and often distracting as appearance. It is more apt to think that the interview structure is part of a continuum, going from being without instruction to being completely structured. [46] however, the structure is often treated as having only two categories (i.e., structured versus unstructured), with many researchers finding that one approach is too simple.

Unstructured

The most structured interview, or one that does not include a good number of standardization items, is the most popular form of an interview today. The unstructured interview is generally considered fluid; the interviewer can exchange or change questions as he sees fit, and different interviewers cannot evaluate or mark a candidate's answers in the same way. There are also no current guidelines on how the interviewer and the interviewee should interact before, during, or after the interview. The unstructured interview essentially allows the interviewer to conduct the interview as they see fit.

Since unstructured interviews may change depending on who the interviewer is, it is no surprise that unstructured interviews are generally preferred by interviewers. Researchers tend to build confidence in their ability to properly assess respondents, detect whether candidates falsify their answers, and based on their judgment of whether the person is a good candidate for the job. The unstructured interview allows researchers to do this more freely. Research suggests, however, that unstructured interviews are, in fact, highly reliable or inconsistent across interviews. This means that two interviewers interviewing the same person may not agree and view the candidate in the same way, even if they were in the same interview with that candidate. Often, researchers conducting unstructured interviews do not identify high-quality candidates for the position. See the section on interview structure topics for further discussion.

Structured

The structure of the interview is the extent to which the interviews are identical and are conducted in the same way among the candidates. Also called guided, systematic or structured interviews, the structured interview intends to do the content (the processed information and the administration of the interactions) and the evaluation (how the candidate is classified), whatever the candidate. Interviewees more specifically, researchers generally provide 15 items that can be used to conduct the interview content and the similar assessment process. The degree of structure of an interview is often seen as the degree to which these elements are included in the interview.

Content structure:

Make sure the questions are relevant to the job, as indicated by a job analysis

Ask all respondents the same questions

Limit follow-up or follow-up requests that researchers can make

Ask better questions, such as behavior description questions

Have a longer interview

Check out the auxiliary information available to respondents, such as cvs

Do not allow candidates' questions during the interview.

Evaluation structure:

Evaluate each answer instead of making an overall assessment at the end of the interview.

Use anchored rating scales (for example, see bars)

Ask the interviewer for detailed notes.

Ask more than one interviewer to see each candidate (ie having panel interviews)

Ask the same interviewer to rate each candidate

Do not allow candidate discussions among interviewers.

Training seekers

Use the statistical procedures to create an overall interview score

Several studies have shown that using these elements to design the interview increases the interviewee's ability to identify the best interpreters. As mentioned earlier, the structure of an interview is structured on a structured scale, but it is not clear which structural elements should be included before it can be considered "structured". Some researchers argue that the inclusion of at least some, but not all, elements of the interview should be considered "semi-structured." others have tried to create levels of structure, such as the four levels of structure of huffcutt, Culbertson and Weyhrauch, which indicate varying degrees of standardization at each level. Although it is difficult to say exactly what a structured interview is, structured interviewing is generally considered more preferred than unstructured organizational interviews if a precise and consistent measure of a candidate is desired.

Types of job interviews:

1. Telephone interview

For most maximum employers, this is the first type of job interview they conduct in their process.

The aim of the phone screen is to decide if you can speak to the curriculum in front of you, particularly in terms of training, experience, and qualifications for the position.

While it is always important to stay friendly, facts are essential on this home screen. don't forget to answer the call from a quiet place and prepare sections of your cv that are perfectly suited to the needs of work and business.

In addition to questions about your qualifications and experience, you should also look for questions about your job search, what you are looking for, reasons you want a new job, and so on.

In general, expect questions about the reasons for your job search and what you want for your next job.

Many employers also ask questions about your desired salary, so be prepared for that!

Be sure to search LinkedIn to see what your phone interview is about. Be it human resources or recruitment, expect more general questions (about your research, your motivation, etc.).

If there is a recruiter or a technician, be ready to answer these types of questions!

Finally, prepare enough questions to ask the interviewer.

2. Face-to-face interview

The face-to-face interview is usually done behind the screen of the phone.

This is where employers evaluate whether you are fit for the corporate culture while asking to confirm the results from the phone screen. (let your skills and experience be combined, etc.)

Your last goal? Build relationships, show that you are in a perfect culture and that you understand their pain clearly and clearly. Your best chance of success is to concentrate, answer questions, and not be distracted.

In addition to practicing excellent interview responses, be sure to work on your language and body confidence.

3. Video interview

The following type of job interview is sometimes done instead of a telephone interview.

This is also sometimes done after having your phone interview ... Instead of a face-to-face interview, you are looking for a job in a new city or a new state.

In most cases, they still want to see you face-to-face, but they could do a telephone interview followed by a video interview before choosing to air for the final stage.

The interviewer needs to determine if you are a good candidate in this type of job interview to make sure you have the expertise, experience, and qualifications required to perform your position well.

From a content perspective, treat this as an in-person interview. Point to a picture with good lighting (make sure your face is not drowned) and a clean background (no shake) and make sure the volume is working and not too high or too soft.

Be prepared to look at the camera (not the screen) in a way that makes eye contact, and be sure to close all applications and change your bells and whistles so that they are not inadvertently activated during the conversation.

Also practice your general body language, as you would for an in-person interview.

Finally, be prepared for the worst-case scenario (technical difficulties) keeping your phone handy in case you need to call in the event of a video connection failure.

4. Group interview

Group or panel interviews can be stressful because many members of the company often interview you simultaneously.

It's not easy, but try to keep eye contact with the person asking the question. However, when it comes to responding or returning with a question of your own, make eye contact with everyone, as you would when presenting to a crowd.

In general, treat this like any face-to-face interview, but prepare for more questions, since you will meet many people at the same time.

Panel interviews can save a lot of time and allow a company to do more interviews and less time. They are becoming more common, so make sure you are ready for this interview format.

Finally, before leaving the interview, ask all business letters to write these thank you letters. Having business cards will also be helpful if you do not hear comments for a week or two and you need to keep up with the employers.

5. One-way software interview

This is relatively new compared to other types of job interviews.

The digital interview allows a company to select questions and read through the candidate's voice recognition software, which is located in front of a camera that records everything. A highly technological format: data analysis and cognitive adjustment are also integrated into the mix and used to vote the candidate.

In addition to making time for the recruiter and mobilization manager, many view digital interviewing as a tool to level the sportive field and eliminate human biases regarding diversity, inclusion, and equity.

To prepare for this type of interview, be sure to place the camera slightly above your face to look for and avoid the appearance of having 2 chins. As in the online interview, choose a place free of distraction and disorder. Stay with short answers and make sure you are passionate, not flat, varying yours and smiling.

Different types of interviews call different game plans: the types and duration of responses to their level of preparation. Understanding the reasoning or final purpose behind each format, and preparing it properly, will give you the best chance of a successful interview.

6. Coffee meeting

In many cases, coffee flips replaced the first formal meeting at the office.

It's not uncommon to talk while having coffee with recruiters who are filling various vacancies or employing managers who do not have room to fill, but who have not yet found job posting or official posting.

So how do you prepare for this type of interview? Even if the place is calm, be sure to do your due diligence and investigate business and industry.

Get ready with an elevator speech that explains how perfect it is for any potential role.

Dress in casual business clothes (here's an article about what to wear during an interview) and bring along several copies of a printed resume. You never know when you'll need an extra copy or two and you better be prepared for this type of interview.

Finally, bring a pen and a notecard. You never want to see the page during your interview, but you can spend 5 to 10% of your time taking notes. Ask the researcher in advance if it is acceptable to bring them. (I like to ask right away after shaking hands. You might say, "I brought a pen and a notecard. Is it okay if you bring this with us?")

They will say yes 99% of the time.

CONVINCING INTERVIEWER YOU ARE THE RIGHT CHOICE

Convincing them you're right for the job
Success in interviews is not as difficult as many people think. With proper preparation and a little practice, most people who are afraid of interviewing can learn to excel. The essential thing to remember is that good interview performance is a learned process. Highly effective respondents were not born with interview skills; rather, learn what to say, how to say, and how to behave during an interview.
Common interview mistakes

We all made mistakes in the interview, and most of us left the interview thinking about all the wonderful things we forgot to talk about and all the things we shouldn't have said. But the most essential thing about mistakes is to learn from them, and not repeat them. Here are some common mistakes in the interview:

Do not speak clearly. Often, because of anxiety and the desire to say things perfectly, we try too hard and turn what should be simple phrases into complicated fool. Simple language is always the most effective. Avoid trying to appear informed by using jargon or complex sentences.

Without being aware of your body language. Many interviewees succeeded in alienating the seeker because they paid little or no attention to their body language. Body language is a very powerful communicator, and if you don't use it effectively, you will definitely be at a major disadvantage. Eye contact, sitting posture, and facial expressions are very important aspects of the interview and should be considered prior to the interview.

Do not control these nerves. Sometimes people leave their nerves out of control so much that they cannot get in touch and even forget their answers. Feelings of anxiety before and during an interview are popular. In fact, a touch of courage can be a great thing. But you should not be the victim of debilitating nerves. By reading this book, you will gradually learn to reduce anxiety.

Give no suitable examples. If you don't give examples or give inappropriate examples, it will be a disaster. Before the interview, it is necessary to think about relevant examples of what you have achieved and how you have achieved these achievements. Saying you get something without being able to save with specific examples will only give you a letter of rejection. Your examples should be easy to understand, follow a logical sequence, and match the needs of employers. None of this happens without preparation.

Try too much to please the interviewer. While it is essential to build relationships and trust during the interview, few interviewers appreciate respondents outperforming their behavior. Gift behaviors are generally considered to be a form of deception and carry little weight; in fact, it can undermine your efforts to build trust.

There's nothing wrong with you

You've probably made at least some of the errors listed above. It is very important to understand that such mistakes are common. In other words, there is nothing wrong. In the vast majority of cases, bad interview results are due to the very nature of the interview: it is the interview process that is to blame.

Therefore, an awareness of the basic nature of the interview is the first step in a step-by-step process through which you can significantly improve your performance. A good starting point is to ask yourself, "what do you need to convince the interviewer that you are the most adequate person for the job?" one can summarize the answer to this question in four parts: right preparation;

Understanding the things that are important to interviewers;

Practicing your answers;

Perseverance.

Correct preparation

The quality of your performance during an interview will largely depend on your preparation. If you do not prepare well, you will certainly not succeed at your best. In some cases, this will mean poor performance, which can contribute to the erosion of your confidence.

Even if you are fortunate enough to be the preferred candidate and are almost assured to win the job simply, you should always take the time to prepare them, because the more successful, the more likely you are to negotiate better pay, and often the difference of money. It can be substantial.

We've all heard about talking about never having prepared an interview in his life and having done well. Although this view is not inactive, closer inspection will generally reveal that these people were:

Lucky, that is, in the right place at the right time;

Well connected

Working in a favorable labor market where there was a high demand for employees associated with low supply;

Ask for good jobs in your comfort zone, that is, do not strive to improve your position; where

Requires internal jobs and competes mainly with external candidates.

The case for preparation

The argument for preparing for an interview becomes compelling when you think about the basic nature of the interview. Not only is it supposed to be sold in a competitive environment, but it also has to compress voluminous and often complex information into clear, highly articulated responses that stay away from any negative implications and contain the information the interviewer wants to hear. Unsurprisingly, people's stress levels increase. But it doesn't stop there. There are three further reasons that make the case for interview preparation even more compelling:

Interviews are rare events that make them unknown and uncomfortable.

Many people find it very difficult to interview themselves because their family and society have conditioned them not to play their trumpets. Making simple statements like "I'm very good at selling xyz" can be an obstacle to overcome.

In most interviews, second place is not enough. It is not just about performing well; it is also a matter of beating everyone.

It is impossible that you are not prepared for a rare and competitive event that requires behaviors that are not commonly used. But, this is exactly what folk do when entering an unprepared interview.

What is incorrect preparation?

A wrong preparation is a preparation that will not optimize your performance during an interview. The generic memory responses that another person has prepared to have a limited value. At best, they can make an overview of what a good answer can be; in the worst case, they only take you. It is necessary to understand that, in most cases, there is no single answer to a question. What may be an excellent answer for one employer may be considered quite ordinary by another. One of the most critical stuff you can do is memorize other people's answers and repeat them in an interview. Repeating the correct answer calls from others can make you look ugly and look a little silly when asking a follow-up question. It offers a lot more sense to prepare your answers.

Benefits of preparation

Take the time to prepare well for an interview:

Improve your confidence levels;

Help answer the questions succinctly, instead of taking forever to make a simple point;

It helps you to know what to say and how to say it;

You help them deal with difficult problems;

You help them avoid saying things that make a negative impression;

Use your skills to build relationships.

Know the important things for researchers.

One of the keys to knowing what he was doing was understanding the interviewer's needs. Once you know the things that are necessary to the researchers, preparing for the interview suddenly becomes much clearer and much more maneuverable.

The vast majority of researchers, whether they know it or not, want to hear three things from you. In fact, almost all interview questions are reduced to these three key generic questions:

Can you do the job? That is, do you have the skills, knowledge, experience, or potential to do well at work? Most interviewers spend most of the interviewing questions on this topic. They want to know what you did, how you did it, and what the results are. In the event that you have not finished a particular table, try to determine your potential for doing the job.

Am i the kind of person I can work with? Another way to ask this question is: do you adapt to the existing culture of the organization? Or in the case of small organizations: do you get along with the leader? Although researchers generally spend much less time on this topic, it is vitally important, because no one wants to work with someone who does not like them, even if they can do the same.

Work

Am i motivated in other words, what levels of energy and dynamism contribute to this position? You may not even be asked about your motivation levels, but it is not at your own risk. As we all know, highly inspired employees are highly sought after by employers, and with good reason.

There are two important benefits to knowing that researchers are very interested in these three generic questions and that the vast majority of the questions they can ask to belong to one or more of these categories. First, it guides you to prepare your answers (much of this book is based on answering these three key questions). Instead of using a lot of time reviewing randomly selected questions in the hope that you have prepared the correct answers, understanding the importance of the three key generic questions provides a guide and platform for their preparation. In summary, you can plan your preparation around the following questions:

Your skills, expertise, and experience—can you do the job?

Your personal qualities—are you the sort of person they can work with?

Your motivation levels

Secondly, it provides a useful way to answer questions during the current interview. By combining interview questions into one or more of the three general categories of questions, your answers gain structure and direction more clearly because you know what the purpose of the questions is. By learning to recognize the true intent of a question, minimize the chances of giving a wrong answer and/or relief.

Practice

The third aspect of convincing a researcher who is the best person for the job is practice. Unfortunately, there are no shortcuts to developing excellent interview skills. Once you have prepared your answer, you should sit down and practice as much as possible. The more you train, the better you go. As the old saying goes, "success is part talent and nine-part persistence." how you practice depends on you. Stand in front of the mirror, sitting on your couch, walking around your room, or driving your car, but avoid practicing in front of your head!

Practicing your answers aloud

It's important to practice your answers aloud, rather than just mentally repeating them. This is because the human brain makes the distinction between speaking and thinking and that part of the speaking brain needs to be stimulated. Thinking about your answers during an interview will never take you away unless the interviewer is a mind reader.

Get some feedback

Ideally, you should do your practice in real interviews. The more you participate in the interview, the better, even if you have to attend job interviews that do not really interest you. After the interview, assuming that you are not the winning candidate, call the interviewer, and ask for comments on their behavior. Some interviewees are happy to provide these comments; however, many prefer not to do so because they find it threatened and a waste of time. These people will completely avoid or provide you with such moderate comments that will be virtually useless.

In some illustrations, you may not be able to solve this problem; however, you can increase your chances of receiving honest feedback by making interviewers as comfortable as possible. You can do this a) by ensuring that you only want five minutes of your time, and b) saying that the only reason they seek comment is to improve the performance of future interviews.

Mock interviews

If you cannot get as many interviews as you want, it is a good idea to organize mock interviews with someone you can work with. The more you look at a real situation, the more you will earn with it. An effective way to conduct wrong interviews is to play a role and stay here throughout the interview. No distractions, not even above all for never getting started. If possible, avoid asking your assistants questions; let me find you. If your assistants can't do it, ask them a few questions and ask them to choose the ones they want. The important thing is for you to get used to answering unexpected questions. Also, if you think your assistant can provide honest comments on your show, feel free to ask. You never know what you can learn. It's usually the small things that make a huge difference. But watch out for the positive comments too. The assistant is probably a friend, and friends are well known for avoiding the negatives.

Perseverance

The most dangerous thing you can do when you think about improving your interview is to make it all seem too difficult. The waivers invariably do not get anywhere. They certainly don't get a good job and they don't have a great career. On the other hand, people who chase often acquire valuable information simply because they have the resistance to survive.

People we admire are often those who face seemingly insurmountable obstacles, but instead of giving up, they quietly decide to overcome. On the different side of the coin, the folk we respect least are the ones who start things forever without end. They are generally the same people who make big statements but end up providing little or nothing. A common feature that chronic smokers tend to have is low self-esteem: they don't really believe in themselves. And if you do not believe in yourself, others generally do not believe in you; it's not a good place to be when trying to persuade researchers to believe in your skills. Here are people you often hear say things like: "it's too difficult", "I can't learn this", "what others think", and so on. They are also people who always complain but do not seem to take any action because there is always an excuse.

You should not be chronically or overwhelmed with low self-esteem to stop working on your interview skills; there may be a number of other reasons. However, if you are reading this book, there is a good chance that improving your interviewing skills is an essential priority in your life and therefore should not be easily forgotten when you think you may be among those who intend to stop smoking, here's a quick exercise that can help you save a step or two.

Neurolinguistic programming

Based on neurolinguistic programming (NLP), this application is intended to influence how you feel. People often ask why they associate negative feelings with what they do. Persecutors have the power to feel good about their actions, no matter how tired or unconstructive these actions may seem to others. If you can feel good about improving your interviewing skills, chances are quitting smoking is the last thing you think about. Next time you feel like planting, you can find a quiet place and follow these steps:

Close your eyes and imagine that you performed extremely well in an interview. Take your time to view this image in as much detail as possible. Imagine the faces of enthusiastic seekers, noting how attentive and impressed they are with answers. Immerse yourself in the experience. Pay attention to details, including sounds, smells, colors, temperature, etc. Above all, catch the feeling of success. Don't stop. The more you feel, the stronger the exercise.

Continue repeating this exercise until you get this feeling of excitement. You may be able to generate more enthusiasm by imagining yourself in your new job. Imagine how good it will feel to win a great job. Imagine receiving all those important phone calls to inform you of your success. Imagine all the things you dreamed of being able to do. The key to this exercise is to create a great feeling that accompanies the success of an interview. Your only limitation is your imagination.

Once you have captured that feeling, the next step is to recreate it when you need it, in other words, when you want to stop. An effective way to recreate the feeling of emotion is to configure what NLP calls an anchor. An anchor is a motive that triggers the desired feelings when you want them. An anchor can be anything you do, say, or imagine. Action anchors generally work better. For example, you could cross your fingers or jump in the air or pull your ears. No matter what, as long as you can easily do it whenever you want and unleash the desired feelings. Whenever you are affected by the scourge of quitting smoking, use your anchor, and let your ability to determine your feelings do the rest.

Summary of key points
Due to their nature, interviews are inherently difficult. Making mistakes during an interview is something everyone does. The fabulous news is that

we can overcome our mistakes with proper preparation, practice, and persistence.

Beware of faulty preparation. Avoid memorizing other people's responses. Always prepare yours.

Knowing what employers want to hear during an interview is an excellent starting point to prepare their own responses and simplifies the preparation of the interview. What most employers love to hear can be represented by three key questions:

Are you the kind of person they can work with?

How motivated are you?

Can you do the job?

Get in as much work as you can and always ask for candid feedback.

Determination is everything.

Banish all thoughts of quitting by preparing yourself to associate strong feelings of excitement with imp

IMPORTANT ACTIONS FOR
INTERVIEW SUCCESS

What are the things you want to achieve in your next interview? While most people know that maintenance is important to you and your employer, few job seekers have a clear impression of what they should achieve during these critical minutes. The following page! Describe interview techniques in more detail, but the following will help you quickly understand the most important things to do during an interview.

1. Make a positive impression

Employers rarely hire someone to make a negative or subsequent first impression. These tips can help you make a good idea before and during your interview.

Before the interview

What happens before the interview is very important, although often forgotten. Before you meet potential employers, you often have indirect contact with those who know them. You can also contact the employer directly by email, phone, or correspondence. Each of these contacts creates an impression.

Tip: administrative assistants, receptionists, and other staff you contact talk about their observations to the interviewer, be professional and courteous in all meetings with staff.

There are three ways an interviewer can get an idea before meeting him in person:

The searcher already knows you. An employer may know through previous contacts or from a description of another person. In this condition, your best approach is to acknowledge this relationship, but treat the interview in all other respects as a business meeting.

The interviewer was contacted by email or telephone. Email and phone are important tools for finding a job. The way you deal with these contacts creates an impression, even if the contacts are short. For example, contact by telephone and contact by e-mail give you an impression of your language skills and your ability to present yourself competently; an email will also quickly communicate your level of written communication skills. So, if you organize an interview with your employer, you've already created an impression, probably quite positive.

The day before the interview you must be a call to check your meeting time. Say something like, "Hey, I want to confirm the continuation of our two-hour interview. " get all the addresses you need. This type of call is just another way to show your attention to detail and help communicate the importance you gave to this interview.

The interviewer has read your cv and any other job search correspondence. Prior to most interviews, provide employers with some type of information or documentation that creates an impression. Sending a note, letter, or email in advance often gives the impression that it is well organized. Applications, CVS, and other correspondence sent or emailed in advance allow interviewers to know more about you. If done right, they will help create a positive impression.

PREPARATION AND PLANNING

Importance of planning and preparation

Imagine you have applied for a job you really want. Today, "plop", on the mat, comes to a letter inviting you to an interview. All our congratulations! Until then, everything he did impress the employer. Now that we have a good idea of the principles behind the interview process, we can look more closely at what they say. Planning and preparation will allow you to immerse yourself in the process to give you trust that leads you to entity and success.

A vital part of your preparation for an interview is deciding in advance your vision of yourself, how you view your employer and your ideas on what to do in the workplace. This is especially essential if you are asked to make a presentation during the interview. This part of the interview preparation process could be called research and development:

research work and how it looks, and develop your plan to portray yourself and your strengths.

Your view of yourself

Take some time to think about your work history, especially when trying to understand what your experience will look like when viewed by an employer. Can you easily identify your transferable skills, that is, those who will apply directly to this position? What specifically did you do in your last job in terms of practical activities? It is helpful to make a preliminary list at this point to remember how you spent your time in a previous job. Take some time to study what has been going well in these recent works, what you have gained, and the key skills you have demonstrated.

In addition to being clear about your strengths and abilities, you must be able to explain the holes in your cv or something that is not conventional. For example, you may have had periods when you were not employed or a student. If this is the case, it is very likely that these breaks will be noted and recovered during an interview, so you should be able to discuss your past all without shame. It means taking advantage of the way your time is spent. If he was unemployed, what did he do with his time? Traveling, what have you learned from your experiences in different places? Parking lots and breaks are not necessarily considered bad or unfortunate as you talk about what you have experienced in a positive way, especially underlining what you have learned from it.

How do you see the pattern?

With a large amount of information available in our knowledge economy, there is no excuse for not knowing much about an employer before attending the interview. An organizational website is obviously a good place to start. A useful part of your preparation is to find out as much as possible by answering the following questions:

What products or services does this employer process?

What are the stated goals and values or the mission statement of the organization, if any?

If it is a private sector company, what is its performance and who are its main competitors?

This is a non-profit organization, which gives priority to funding agencies and politicians?

How would you describe what kind of organization it is?

What kind of skills are you looking for now?

Can you identify the culture of the organization? What do you think and how do you handle things? How do you feel about working here? There is a huge difference between a traditional and hierarchical institution and a young and dynamic society. Which one do you feel most at home? Why?

Research

The next step in planning is to gather as much information as you can about the vacancy and the organization. You will rarely be invited to an interview without receiving any cliches about the type of candidate required. If the position has been announced and a job description or, at best, a person specification has been sent to you, you are likely to be informed of most areas where you are likely to be questioned.

A job description, as the name implies, details the main job functions and the specification of a person explains the type of person the employer is looking for. These two documents are very useful. Make sure you pay close consideration to the documents you receive at work. The employer took a hard and difficult time to figure out what the job entails. You have to prove that you have got a lot to offer for each of their parts.

Relate your thinking to the research you did when you applied for the job for the first time. You can take advantage of this prior work and plan how your experience can match the skills and experience required for the job. If this does not fit the job description or the specifications of the person, you will find additional points in your favor that can compensate for these shortcomings.

In the past, when there were far fewer job seekers, it was important to carefully review these documents to show that you had the experience and character to find a job. Today, with much more competition, it's not just about paying attention to detail but finding ways to "sell" it. Such an expression seems to apply more to detergent than to man, but it is a good term to use.

Think about advertising any clothes on television. Not even a box of detergent shows up and they tell us to buy. We can show you a washing line full of bright white clothing to show you exactly what the product can do. We have been frequently told that it was washed whiter; from our clothes a pleasant and fresh odor; it is significantly cheaper than its competitors; it comes in a rechargeable package; removes dirt and stains, etc.

Because of all other similar product domains, the message is sent home. But when we look at ads like this, it doesn't seem like the message was too strong; instead, we believe it may be a product we should try. This is the effect we want to create with interviewers by using the time available to promote our positive strengths and attributes.

ANALYZING THE JOB

The job description

By carefully examining the details of the job description, you can see what the employer expects from the employer. Work is sometimes divided into those where certain experience is essential and others where experience is preferred. Ideally, you should follow the following steps:

Work through the job description, taking one section at a time.

Underline or mark words that mention the main work activities (verbs), for example, organize work; prepare budgets; writes reports; dealing with customers

Take approximate notes to demonstrate how you have gained experience in all of these activities;

think of an example of your experience or work experience for everyone.

Transform your raw notes into a written or typographic form that answers questions about how each of the points you highlighted is met.

Review the information you have provided on your application listing, adding other examples, if necessary, to get a lot of different types of evidence to offer.

The person specification

This document is often sent to vacancies in large companies, local authorities, other public sector or public service employers, all of whom have large human resources departments. It contains useful information about the type of person the organization is looking for. Your approach to this information should be the same as the job description:

Study carefully to see which features are essential or preferred for the job and highlight both.

Review each of these in general terms, and see an example of your own experience that shows how your personality fits what is needed. You must provide proof that you have all the features marked as essential for a successful interview. It is a good idea to prepare more than one example if you are requesting a supplement.

Write your answers inappropriate sentences so that you can repeat them for the interview itself.

If you have already filed your application form for this position, review it now to update your report and be able to fully prepare your answers on how to meet the person's specifications.

How to find out more

You can contact the company formally or informally to learn more about them and what they do. For formal contact, I would like to call and speak with the staff manager or local manager. For instance:

"I was immediately invited to an interview with your company/organization and was asking if there was any other information available about your products/services."

There may be a specific question you want to answer, such as:

'Are all your offices based around London?'

Someone is happier not to reveal that they are coming for an interview and just say they are investigating and want information. State-owned companies publish annual reports that contain useful information on recent major projects.

Companies often advertise their products or services in magazines, local and national newspapers, and on the internet. These ads show how the company is presented and tell you what their main products are.

If you are running a certain organization, you can search the internet. Search engines are fast and powerful ways to search for specific information. A good example is www.google.co.uk. You can use it to search for words related to certain types of work or to identify information about a specific employer. Most organizations now have their own website, which describes what they do and how they do it. Paint the employer site that will interview you until you know everything you can about the company. Look carefully at the words and pictures they use to describe themselves. What kind of pictures do they portray? Think carefully about what you see. It will not be enough to say that you have visited the site as planned. You have to draw your own conclusions. Also look at the websites of other similar organizations, or those of their competitors, as you find more useful information from these sources.

For some senior employees, you may be asked to call the company for an informal discussion on the job before submitting the application. If this happens for a job you are considering, you should contact the employer to verify that your application is being taken seriously. However, you must treat this telephone contact as a mini-interview. Examine your cv before you call and consider why you think it might be appropriate, what specifically interests you at work, and, in particular, what you think it has to offer at work. If you have any questions, prepare in advance by using a pencil and paper to take notes during the call.

Thinking about the job

When you are satisfied that you have gathered as much material as possible in the time available, you should begin to think seriously about the topics that may be covered during the interview. For starters, though, consider the following announcement, seen in a local newspaper:

Stock handler

A busy warehouse requires seasonal managers to work in their warehouse to sort and check inventory. Training is provided but a useful experience.

What can we say, of this brief announcement, of the person sought? Even without a job description or a person specification, and without knowing the company name, we can use common sense to deduce the following. The person must be in good shape and in good health to be able to carry stock boxes. There will necessarily be a number of documents and administrations, which involves completing and verifying inventory cards, so the right candidate will need to know how to read and write. Some computer literacy, or at least a desire to learn, will always be helpful. The use of lifting equipment and/or driving ability may also be relevant to this work.

The store will be great if it has its own warehouse, so work is likely to involve working with teams of people. You need someone with a friendly and flexible approach. Accuracy will be important and you should be careful about the value of the goods handled. The candidate must be honest and be able to rely on values.

All of these features and features can be inferred from the brief details in the ad. It might have a much more accurate idea of the person being sought if they were given a job description and a person specification. But even without them, there is no excuse for not thinking about what the employer is looking to do in preparation.

If you are not ready to plan a bit before the event and do not think you can get excited about the vacancy, it may mean that you do not take the job application seriously. Generally speaking, if a job is worth it, it's worth spending time getting ready for it, which means you've reviewed all the information available to find clues to exactly what you're looking for. Trustee this will help you form a profile of the candidate who is most likely to succeed.

Areas of likely questioning

Earlier it was said that an employer would focus on three main problem areas. You certainly know that you will be asked questions about: (a) your qualifications and skills; (b) your past professional experience; and (c) its character or personality. Let's take a nearer look at each of these areas.

 (a) your qualifications and skills

Before you are interviewed, it is necessary to prepare a good cv. This document is useful for interviews and applications, as it should contain a concise list of courses taken and work done. Before the interview, you have to do a background check, especially if you have taken several different courses. The fluctuation of your answers when you are not sure about your field is too obvious to an interviewer and they seem to be unprofessional.

Then you will be completely familiar with what you have studied, and where and when. You almost need to be able to read your cv while you sleep! Therefore, when your training has been requested, the information you need will be easy and concise.

When you are interviewed and asked about your previous education, the employer does not want to hear you read a list of the courses you have taken. Ask why your employer should be interested in such information. The reason is that you want to know what you have learned from your studies. In most cases, therefore, it is more important to review the main topics studied, the projects you have worked on specifically, the exams you have taken, if any, and the parts of the course you have most. **Appreciated or more learned**.

Those who have not taken the exam will also talk about courses taught at school or in college. You have to determine what your favorite subjects were, what lessons benefited the most, and why.

(b) your previous work experience

The same goes for your work experience. All your work and the details of what you have done as the main works will be taken into account. You should not assume that what you have done as a secretary is obvious to an interviewer. Most interviewers will be interested in the specific skills used in the job that could help contribute to the position required.

You may think that all employees file, but what kind of documents do they handle? Are these important documents or legal plans, original letters, or personal information of the client? It can be used to choose things by number instead of alphabetically, or you may have to crucial reference. Have you ever had to retrieve files, work under pressure, or find missing documents? Have you ever used specific computer programmers, answered questions from the public, or been in touch with colleagues from other departments? Were the documents confidential or private or needed special treatment before filing? Coding for ease of recovery?

All of these things might be called transferable skills - skills that you learn or use in one job and that can be transferred to the next. The benefit of an employer must be obvious. Your competence in a field of work, where you can demonstrate your experience, means that you do not necessarily need the training to do the same in the next job.

Again, consider why the interviewer asks these types of questions. The answer is, to see what kind of employee he would do. Therefore, when you work in a particular place it is not as important as what you contributed, as this gives the employer an idea of your skills.

(c) your character or personality

Among the three main areas of interest to an employer, the greatest importance is given to the type of person he is. It happens again and again;

even if a candidate's academic background or previous experience does not match that of his or her competitors, demonstrating certain advantages in terms of personality or character, the candidate succeeds. Why would that be? While a candidate is the type of person who will be integrated into the company and likes his or her job, this person can easily be trained to make up for any lack of skills or experience.

Sharing the vision

There is another aspect that employers have to consider during the interview. It seems that many candidates have the right qualifications, experience, and personality to fill the vacancy. What else could make the difference between the best and the rest? In a recession, employers may discover that they are starting to find some suitable candidates. They will look for ways to choose the people who offer them the most. If candidates can show that they are thinking about the job, especially the contribution they can make and the way they are done, the job cannot succeed.

This requires spending time thinking about the key aspects of the job. What are the organization's strengths and weaknesses from what you can see? What can you discover about the environment in which the company operates? Think about work and organization and try to analyze the factors that might be important.

For example, if the job is vacant in a business company, who are its competitors? What is your image of the product or service you provide? Is there a change in the world that can affect business activity? What about the nature of the specific job in question? What do you think are the more essential characteristics of the job and why? How do you imagine doing the job and what special contribution would you make?

Spending time developing your ideas or your vision for the future of the organization shows your commitment and your interest in the work and the likely added value that you can bring compared to other candidates. Most employers do not have time to think about the specifics of each job in their organization. They want to recruit people who can do the right job by name and bring new ideas and energy to the job. It improves the impression he gives if he can even speak intelligently about his vision of the organization and how he sees his role.

Mind the gap! Covering up your weak spots

We all have something we would prefer if the interviewer doesn't stop. For some, you can spend time in unemployment; for others, it may be something in their past that they would prefer to hide, such as several job changes or having been in a job for too long. Few people have a perfect work history, for various circumstances, such as having a family, poor health, past or present unemployment, incarceration, or detention. Some of us have had rules to take care of family members, maybe elderly parents, or we have taken some time to align the children. You may have left a job in a hurry or you feel that your work history seems uneven and unimportant. Do not think that ignoring these delicate problems will disappear. Gaps or inconsistencies in your cv or application form will be identified and interrogated. You will be able to address all aspects of your trip with confidence and a positive explanation. No employer expects you to navigate through life without problems or difficulties, but you must spend some time preparing the way to qualify and clarify.

The important thing is to reflect and train yourself to close those gaps. Explain the learning, not how you lie, but how to positively present a compelling and convincing explanation of the relevant experience you have gained in the past.

Maximizing your strengths

The best approach is not to cover past experiences, but to present them in a different way. This forces us to make a virtue of the things that have happened to us out of necessity.

Golden rules

1. Always be positive about previous jobs

It's also important to always be positive about every job you've had in the past. Why should it be so vital? Again, let's take a look at it from the perspective of the employer. If an interviewer would be impressed to hear a candidate say how bossy their last employer was? Would it be nice to hear another company fired or slandered by a candidate, or does the employer believe the candidate could say the same about this company in a few years?

Someone who fancies other organizations also creates a sense of security and a negative attitude. No one will be interested in employing such a candidate. A positive candidate and enthusiasm will be preferred.

2. Be enthusiastic and motivated

Nothing attracts people like enthusiasm. The candidate who performs such a function has a great advantage, almost before anything else is said or taken into account. We are all more interested in working with the person who comes in with a good mood and a positive feeling about work every day, rather than with the gray or the problem that is always negative.

3. Capitalise on your strengths

The only thing the interviewer understands about you is what goes into your application or cv and what you will talk about during the interview. So, what you say about yourself gives the impression that the intervener has of you, that is, your ability, experience, and personality. The interviewer will consider you a potential worker or a member of staff; it must mean that everything you have done to this day has led to this work, with this organization, at that moment. Add that your vision of how the work should be managed by now. Irresistible!

Which questions to ask?

Usually, you will be asked at the end of the interview, if you have any questions. Do not feel like asking for something just for fun. An employer's heart will sink if he begins to appear on a long list of questions as soon as the interview is over. Ask only if needed. If you feel you know everything you need to know about the job, it's good to say something like:

"I think you've already covered all the important points, thank you. But if I have any further questions, I'll be in touch with you."

Don't ask about uniforms, vacations, or other practical things. If you are given the job, you will be informed of this type of detail when you begin.

If the compensation has not been mentioned so far, it is not time to raise the issue. You probably wouldn't accept any job without knowing your salary, but once again, you might find once you've received the job offer when you can respond to:

"I love working at the moment, but I'm still unsure of working conditions. Can you tell me exactly what wages and hours are?" "

If you decide to ask the interviewer, it is a good idea to show your general attitude through what he says. Questions about the training opportunity or the possibility of taking more responsibility in the future show that you are willing, thinking about being at work, and wanting to join the organization.

You may ask, "will there be opportunities for more specialized work later?" or "can you tell me a little bit about the personal development you support for your employees?"

Dos and don'ts

Use new technologies and the internet to give you an edge when you search.

Start by consulting what you put into your application; that's what interviewed her.

Think about the type of person your employer will look for.

Don't leave the research until the last minute; you may need more time than you think.

Don't eat if it doesn't seem to fill all the vacancies, it may be exactly what you are looking for.

Remember to prepare examples of all the items you require.

The day of the interview

To make a great impression on the interview day, use these tips:

Get there punctually. Try to schedule many interviews in the same area of the city and in the same amount of time so you don't waste time on excessive travel. Get instructions online (at www.mapquest.com or other similar sources) or ask for instructions from the receptionist to determine how to get to the interview and how long it will take to get there. Allow enough time for traffic or other problems and plan to reach for maintenance 5-10 minutes early.

Check your appearance. Get there early enough to get into the bathroom and correct any toilet issues your trip has caused, such as brown hair. You would be astonished by the number of people who attend the interview with grooming problems, such as disheveled hair or stained lipstick on their teeth. Use mint or gum to be safe. Do not spray perfumes, colognes, or hairspray just prior to the interview, as many people are sensitive to chemicals and perfumes.

Use appropriate behavior in the waiting room. While waiting for the interview to begin, keep in mind that it is important to relax and unwind. Learn from something professional. For example, you can review your notes on the questions you want to ask during the interview, the key skills you want to present, or other interview details. Bring a professional magazine to read or buy one at the front desk. The waiting room may also contain publications from the organization itself that you have not yet seen. You can also use this time to update your daily schedule.

Be prepared if the interviewer is late.

I hope this happens. If you arrive quickly but you have to wait longer than expected, this puts the interviewer in a "gee, sorry, I must" mood. If the interviewer is 15 minutes back, go to the office or administrative assistant and say something like "I still have an appointment today. Think it will be a lot longer before it becomes available (enter the name of interviewer)? " do well, but don't act like you can sit still all day. If you wait more than 25 minutes after the scheduled time, you can ask to postpone the interview until you have fun. Say that is not a problem for you and understand that things are happening. Also, say you want to be sure that Mr. And Mrs. Tal and such do not feel pressured when he or she tells you. Set the new calendar, accept all excuses with a smile, and go out of your way. When you return your interview, the interviewer is likely to apologize and treat you very well.

Pay attention to your dress and appearance. The way you dress and prepare can create a big negative or positive impression, especially during the first seconds of an interview. With so many choices of styles, colors, and other factors, determining the right approach can become quite complex. To avoid complexity, follow this simple rule: it is likely that the interviewer is dressed and puffed up, but only slightly better.

Shake hands and maintain good eye contact. If the employer offers you a hand, shake hands (but not too firmly) with a smile. As absurd as it sounds, a little practice helps. Avoid looking, but look at the interviewer when one of you talks. This will help you focus on what is being said and let the employers you are listening to and have a good social standing.

I am interested. Sit down, lean slightly into your chair and hold your head, looking directly at the interviewer. This position helps you to appear interested and alert.

Eliminates annoying behavior. Try to eliminate any disturbing movement or gesture. A woman from one of my actors was seen on a camcorder constantly playing with her hair. It was only then that he knew he had this distracting behavior. Listen and you may notice that he says "aaahhh" or "ummmmm" often, or says "do you know what I mean?" repeatedly or use other repetitive words or phrases. You can understand, but be careful. Ask your friends or family to help you identify these behaviors.

Pay attention to your voice. If you are gentle by nature, try to increase your volume slightly. Listen to news reporters and other professional speakers who are good role models for volume, speed, and tone. For example, I have a pretty deep voice. I have learned to change my tune by giving presentations so that everyone does not sleep. Your voice and performance will improve as you gain experience and conduct more interviews.

Use the official name of the interviewer as often as possible. Do this especially in the first part of the interview and again when you finish. Do not call the interviewer by name, unless the researcher tells you otherwise.

Play the game of chat for a while. Researchers often comment on the moment, asking if they had trouble reaching or making another joint opening. Be friendly and make some appropriate comments. Don't start your business visit too soon when these informal openings are standard measures of your socializing skills. Smile is not verbal and people will respond more favorably if they smile.

Discuss something personal in the interviewer's office. "I like the office! Have you decorated yourself?" or "I saw the sailboat. Were you sailing?" or "your officer is fantastic! How long have they been here?" the idea here is to explain something that interests you and encourage employers to talk about it? This interest rate is a compliment if your enthusiasm is manifested. This tactic can also give you the opportunity to share something you have in common, so try to choose a topic on which you know something.

Ask some initial questions. Once the pleasant conversation is over, be prepared to steer the interview in the direction you want to go. This process can occur within one minute of your first greeting but is more likely to take up to five minutes.

2. Communicate your skills

If you have created a positive rational self-image so far, someone will now be interested in the reasons why you should consider putting it together. This round-tour conversation usually lasts 15 to 45 minutes, and many consider it the most important and difficult task of any job search.

Fortunately, when you read this book, you have many advantages over the average job-seeker:

You will know what kind of job you require.

You will know what skills are needed to do well in that job.

You will have those very skills.

All you have to do is discuss these three things directly and completely answering questions from an employer.

3. Use control statements to your advantage

A control statement is a statement that you make that becomes the route map for the direction of the conversation (interview). While you may think that you are at the mercy of the interviewer, You have a certain ability to set the interview course, from the topic to the approach you want.

For example, it could mean something as simple as, "I want to tell you what I've done, what I like to do, and why I think it would be a good combination with your organization." your statement of control can come at the beginning of the interview if things seem unclear after the chat or at any time during the interview when you feel the focus is far from the points you want to emphasize.

Some other key statements and questions to ask at the beginning of an interview:

"How did you begun in this type of career?"

"I want to hear more about your organization's doing. Would you care to tell me what?"

"I have got a background in _____ and am interested in how I might be Regarded for a position in a Company such as yours."

"I have 3years of experience more than two years of training in the field of _____. I am actively finding a job and know that you Possibly do not have openings now, But I would like to see potential opportunities. Maybe if I told you small things about myself, you could give me some Technique of whether you will have an interest in me."

4. Answer problem questions well

Every employer is trying to figure out the problems or limits that might be contributing to your work. However, according to employers in the northwestern university Endicott report, about 80% of all job applicants cannot answer one or more problematic interview questions correctly. Everyone has a problem and employers are trying to find yours. Wait for him. Suppose you have been unemployed for three months. This can be considered a problem unless it can provide a good reason. Provides more tips for answering problematic questions and other key questions that may be asked.

5. Ask good questions

Many employers ask for an interview sometime if you have an application. The way you react affects their assessment of you. So, be ready to ask insightful questions about the organization. Good topics to discuss are:

● the competitive conditions in which the organization operates.

● executive management styles

● what obstacles does the organization think of achieving its goals?

● how the goals of the organization have changed over the last three to five years.

As a common rule, it is not wise to ask questions about compensation, benefits, or other similar things at this time. That's because it tends to make you more involved in what the company can do for you, rather than what you can do for it. Without questions, you seem passive or something else, more than curious and interested.

6. Assist employers to know why they should hire you

Even if the interviewer never says it directly, the question in his mind is still "why should you employ yourself instead of someone else?" the best answer to this question is providing benefits to employers, not you. A correct answer shows that you can help an employer make more money by improving efficiency, reducing costs, increasing sales, or solving problems (getting to work, improving customer service, organizing one or many employers ask for an interview at a time if you have an application. The way you react affects their assessment of you. So, be ready to ask insightful questions about the organization. Good topics to discuss are:

● the competitive conditions in which the organization operates.

● executive administration styles

● what obstacles does the organization think of achieving its goals?

● how the goals of the organization have changed over the last three to five years.

- do not allow maintenance to take too long. Most interviews doest not take more than 30 to 60 minute. Unless the researcher asks otherwise, think about staying for no more than an hour. Pay attention to the clues of the researchers, such as watching a clock or playing cards, which are ready to end the interview.
- summarize the key points of the interview. Use your judgment here and be brief! Review the main issues raised in the employer interview. You can skip this step if the time is short.
- if you have a problem, repeat its resolution. No matter what you think a particular researcher might see as a reason for not employing you, turn to him, and present the reasons why he does not see it as a problem. If you are unsure of what the interviewer thinks, be direct and ask, "Is there anything in me that worries you or that may prevent you from employing me?" however, do your best to respond to them.
- check your strengths for this job. Enable the opportunity to present once again the skills you have regarding this particular job. Just highlight your strengths and keep it short.
- if you won't work, ask. If you want the job, tell me why. Employers are more inclined to employ someone they know is enthusiastic about the job, so let them know if you are. Ask when you can get started. This question may not always be suitable, but yes, yes, do so.

The call back close

This approach to finishing an interview takes some bravery, but it does work. Say it a few times, and use it to get more confident with it in your early interviews.

1. Thanks for to name of the interviewer. As they shake their hand, say, "thank you (Mr. Or ms. Or ms._____) for your time today."

2. Express concern. Depending on the situation, discuss your interest in the job, organization, service, or product by saying, "I'm very interested in the plans we've been working through today," or "I'm very interested in your organization." it seems an interesting place to work." or, if there is a task opening and you want it, say confidently, "I'm certainly interested in this position."

3. Tell us about your busy schedule. Say: "the next few days I'm busy, but..."

4. Arrange a date and reason to call back. Your goal is to leave a reason to get back in touch and make arrangements for a particular day and time to do so. Say, for instance, "I am sure I have questions.

When would it be the best time I could get back with you?" note that I said "when" instead of "is it ok to..." because asking when doesn't easily allow a "no" response. Choose a specific day and the best time to call.

5. Say good-bye.

8. Follow up after the interview

The interview is over, you've made it home and now you're just sitting back and waiting, right? Incorrect. Successful follow-up efforts will make a huge difference when it comes to getting a job offer done by eligible candidates.

Follow-up, as I say in this book, can make the difference between being unemployed or underemployed and having the job you want quick. For more information on successful follow-up via telephone.

INTERVIEW QUESTIONS

HOW TO ANSWER INTERVIEW QUESTIONS

#3 simple step process for answering most interview questions

There are thousands of questions you might ask in an interview, and there is no way to memorize a "correct" answer for everyone, especially not the day before the interview. Interviews are not simply so because they are often conversational and informal. It often happens often

For these reasons, developing an approach to responding to an interview request is far more important than memorizing a standardized response.

I have developed a technique called a three-step process that you can use to form an effective answer to most interview questions:

1. Understand what is really needed. Most of the questions concern your abilities and personalities. These questions involve: "can we depend on you?"; "am i easy to understand?"; and "am i a good

worker?" demand can also be linked to whether you have the knowledge and training to do the job if you are insured.

2. Answer the question briefly without prejudice. A correct answer to a question should recognize the facts of your situation and present them as an advantage instead of a disadvantage.

3. Answer the real question by giving your related skills. An effective answer to any interview question must answer the question directly, which also demonstrates your capacity to do the job well.

Let's use this to show you how to use the three-step process to answer a specific question:

Question: "We were in need of someone with more experience than you seem to have in that area. Why should we find you better qualifications over others?"

The following sections illustrate how one person might use the three-step process to create an answer to this question.

Step 1: get full knowledge of what is really being asked

This question is frequently posed in a less direct manner but is also a concern of employers. To answer it, you need to remember that employers often hire people with better credentials who represent themselves well in an interview over those.

Your best shot is to highlight any personal qualities you possess that might offer an employer an advantage. The person needs to know if you've got something that will help you compete with a more experienced worker.

Okay, right, you? Were you a toiler? Will you know quickly? Would you have intense preparation or practical experience? Would you have an expertise that can be moved to this role from other activities? To answer this question it is important to know beforehand what skills you have to give.

Step 2: Answer the question Shortly in a non-damaging way

For instance, the following answer answers the question without undermining the chances of the person getting the job: "I'm curious to know there are people who have more years of experience or better qualifications.

I have four years of combined training and practical experience using the latest methods and techniques, however.

I'm open to new ideas because my training is recent, and I'm used to working hard and learning fast."

Step 3: answer the real question by Going to present your related skills

Although the above answer answers the question appropriately and briefly, you can continue with additional details that focus on the key skills required for the job:

"as you know, I had a full-time job and a family responsibility during my studies. In those two years, I had an excellent record of attendance at work and school, missing just one day in two years. .i also received two merit increases, and my grades were in

25 percent of my class. To do this, I had to learn how to organize my time and set priorities. I worked hard to prepare for this new area. Professional and I am ready to continue working to establish myself. The position you hold is what I am ready to do. I am ready to work harder than the next person because I want to continue to learn and do exceptional work. After my studies are finished, I can now devote my full attention to this work. ""

This answer presents the skills needed to do well in any job. This job search seems reliable. He also gave examples of situations in which he had used the skills required in other contexts. That's a good answer

The prove-it technique

The three-step process is important to understand that the often-asked interview question is an attempt to explore the underlying information. You can provide this information by effectively using the prove-it technique in four steps:

1. Present a concrete example: people tell stories and memories. Saying that you have a skill is not as powerful as describing a situation in which you have to use that skill. The example should add enough details to make sense of who, what, what, where, when, and why.

2. Quantify: when possible, use the numbers to provide a basis for what you've done. For example, it includes the number of customers served, the percentage of fee surplus, the amount of mourning

you were responsible for, or the number of new accounts you created.

3. Emphasize results: it is important to provide data on the positive results you have achieved. For example, you could indicate that sales increased 3% over the previous year or that profits increased by 50%. Use numbers to quantify your results.

4. Make the connection: while the link between your example and good work may seem obvious, make sure it's clear to the employer. A simple statement is often enough to get this.

If you do extensive work to finish an activity, it should be easy enough to provide evidence to support the skills you discussed in an interview.

TYPES OF INTERVIEW QUESTIONS
Brainteasers
 panel interview questions
Behavioral interview questions
Experience-based interview questions
Competency-based interview questions
Communication interview questions
Salary interview questions
Opinion based interview questions
Trap interview questions
Traditional interview question
Hypothetical interview questions
INTERVIEW QUESTIONS AND ANSWERS

Common interview questions and answers
1. Tell me about yourself.

Tip: to get to know you, your interviewees will probably start with a question about yourself and your history. Start by providing them with an overview of your current position or activities, then provide the most important and relevant highlights from your history that will make you most qualified for that role.

Example: "I actually work as the assistant to three of the five members of the company's executive team, including the CEO. I've developed the ability to predict roadblocks and create effective alternative plans from my 12 years of experience as an executive assistant. My biggest gratitude to any executive is my ability to work independently, freeing up their time to concentrate on business needs.

It's obvious you're looking for someone who understands the complexities of handling a busy day for the CEO and is willing to proactively address issues. As someone with an eye for organization and a drive to organize, I thrive to make sure that every day has a clear plan and that every plan is clearly communicated.

" visit interview question for more information on answering this question: "tell me about yourself."

2. How would you describe yourself?

Tip: when an interviewer asks you to speak about yourself, they're looking for information on how your strengths and characteristics match the skills they think are necessary to succeed in the role. Provide, where possible, quantifiable results to show how you use the best attributes to drive performance.

Example: "as a security officer, I would say I am vigilant, attentive, and committed to ensuring safe, secure, and organized environments. I got a 99 percent against the team average in my last incident response rating, which has been about 97 percent for the past three years. I like to be thorough, to document every incident. I'm also a lifelong learner, always on the lookout for the latest security equipment and building patrol techniques. I often make suggestions for managing security improvements and changes because my motivation comes from making a meaningful contribution.

" visit interview question for more on answering this question: "how would you describe yourself?"

3. What makes you unique?

Tip: employers often ask this question to figure out why you might be more eligible than other candidates they interview. To reply, focus on why you would help the employer by hiring. Because you don't know the other applicants, it can be difficult to think about your response regarding them. Addressing why your background makes you work well will let employers know why your skills and characteristics make you well prepared.

Example: "it is my perspective of having spent four years in retail that makes me special. Because I've had first-hand experience with questions, suggestions, and concerns from shoppers about shopping, I know what customers need. I know what it requires to create a positive consumer experience because I have had direct interaction, working directly with customers in person."

visit interview question for more detail on answering this question: "what makes you unique?"

4. Why do you want to work here?

Tip: interviewers also pose this question as a way to assess whether or not you have taken the time to study the business and understand why you find yourself a good fit. The best method to prepare for that problem is to do your homework and learn about this workplace's products, services, mission, history, and culture. Mention in your reply the company aspects that appeal to you and fit with your career goals. Explain why you are in an organization looking for such things.

Example: "I am talking about the mission of the organization to help college grads pay off their student loan debt. I was in that position and I would love to have the opportunity to work with a company that is making a difference. Finding a company with a supportive working environment and values aligned with my own remained a priority during my job search and this company ranks at the top of the list."

for more information on answering this question, please visit the interview question: "why do you want to work here?"

5. What interests you about this role?

Tip: like the previous question, hiring managers also include this question to ensure that you understand the position and give you a chance to highlight your applicable skills. This can be useful to equate the work specifications with your skills and experience in addition to reading the job description thoroughly. Pick some things you really enjoy or excel in, and concentrate on those in your response.

Example: "This motivates me to strive for excellence in all I do and make a significant disparity in the lives of my patients and their families. I look forward to seeing their response when we achieve a positive outcome that will permanently change their lives. Like a young boy's family, we handled last year— he had undergone rapid weight gain and indications of depression at age eight. His parents described him as an ordinarily joyful child, but in his typical schedule, he now seemed disengaged and uninterested. In the end, we determined it was hypothyroidism, which is controllable with medication, of course. The boy is well adjusting to the treatment and has gone back to his happy self. That's the reason became a nurse and why I am pursuing a position in pediatrics.

" visit interview question for more information on answering this question: "why are you interested in this position?"

6. What motivates you?

Tip: employers ask this question to assess their level of concussion and make sure their sources of motivation match the role. To answer, be as precise as feasible, provide specific examples, and win your response to the publication.

Example: "making a real difference in the lives of patients and their families motivates me to strive for excellence in everything I do. I can't wait to see my patient's reactions when we get a positive outcome that will change their life forever. That's why I became a nurse and was looking for a pediatric role. """

visit interview question for more on answering this question: "what motivates you?" (for example)

7. What are you passionate about?

Tip: like the previous motivation issue, employers may ask what you're passionate about to get a better knowledge of what drives you and what you care about most. This can help them both to understand whether you're a good fit for the role and whether it fits in with your bigger objectives. To respond, pick something you're truly passionate about, clarify why you're passionate about it, give examples of how you've followed that passion, and link it back to the job.

Example: "as an accomplished, service-oriented professional with over a decade of boutique salon experience, I excel in creating a welcoming environment for all consumers and delivering the highest quality skincare services. My specific training and strong interpersonal skills have helped me develop long-term, trusting relationships that will help build a loyal customer base. Some of my customers have been with me right from the start —

more than 10 years now. Such relationships are the reason I'm excited about going to work every day.

" visit interview question for more on answering this question: "what's your passion for?"

8. Why are you leaving your current job?

Tip: there are several excuses to get out of work. Prepare a thoughtful response that gives faith to your interviewer that you are serious about leaving this job. Focus more on the future and what you expect to achieve in your next position rather than dwelling on the negative part of your current or previous role.

Example: "I am viewing for an opportunity that gives me the ability to build stronger, longer-term customer relations. The selling process is so quick in my current role, that I don't spend as much time developing a relationship with my customers as I would like. Relationship-building is one of the reasons I have chosen a sales career, and I look forward to working with a company where that is a top priority."/

For more information on answering this question, please visit the interview question:" why are you searching for a job?

9. What are your biggest strengths?

Tip: This question provides you an opportunity to explore your technical as well as soft skills. To reply, share your strengths and personal characteristics and then link them back to the position you are interviewing for.

Example: "I am a problem-solver of course. I consider digging deep and uncovering answers to problems exciting — it's like solving a puzzle... It's something that I've always excelled at and I enjoy. Much of product development is about seeking innovative solutions to difficult issues, which is what first drew me to this career path."

Visit the interview question for more detail on answering this question: "what are your strengths and weaknesses?"

10. What are your greatest weaknesses?

Tip: discussing your shortcomings in an atmosphere where you are supposed to reflect on your successes may feel awkward. However, if answered correctly, revealing your shortcomings will demonstrate you are self-aware and want to get better at your job on an ongoing basis—traits that are highly appealing to many employers. Remember to begin with the weakness, then address the steps you have taken to improve. You finish your comment on a positive note this way.

Example: "I had noticed earlier in my career that because I was so enthusiastic about my job, I continued to say' yes' when I was meant to say' no.' at one point I ended up so surprised by my workload, taking on so many tasks, that I worked at nights and weekends. This was stressful, and the stress influenced the quality of my production. I understood that this was counterproductive and I began using task management techniques to set higher expectations for myself and my teammates.

"visit interview question for more detail on addressing this question:" what are your greatest weaknesses? "

11. What are your goals for the future?

Tip: hiring managers also inquire about your potential plans to decide whether you are looking for a long-term commitment with the organization or not. This question is often used to determine your ambition, your goals for your career, and your ability to plan ahead. The best way to handle this problem is to determine your current career direction and how that position can help you achieve your ultimate goals.

Example: "I want to continue to grow my marketing skills over the next few years. One of the reasons I work for a fast-growing startup company is that I can wear a lot of hats and work with a lot of different departments. . I feel that this experience will help me to achieve my ultimate goal of one day leading a marketing department."

Visit the interview question for more information on answering this question: "what are your future goals?"

12. Where would you be in the next 5years?

Tip: knowing how you envision your future life will help employers understand whether the position and business direction suits your personal development goals. To respond, give general ideas about the skills you want to build, the types of roles you want to be in, and the things you want to have accomplished.

Example: "I would like to be an industry expert in my field in five years, able to train and mentor students as well as entry-level designers alike. I would also like to gain advanced user experience as a well-rounded consultant collaborating on large-scale projects with design and marketing teams that make a difference for both the business and the global community.

visit interview question for more detail on answering this question: "where would you see yourself in 5years time?

13. Can you tell me about a hard work situation and how you overcame it?

Tip: This question is often used to determine how well you are doing under pressure, as well as your ability to solve problems. Keep in mind that stories are more unforgettable than facts and figures, so consider "showing" instead of "telling." It's also a great opportunity to show the human side and how you're ready without being asked to go that extra mile.

Illustration: "it was the first day of the two-week break of my manager and the highest-paid customer of our agency threatened to quit because he didn't get the personalized support he was promised. I've spent my lunch hour with him on the phone, talking about his concerns. We have even been brainstorming ideas for his next campaign. He was so thankful for his personal attention that he signed another deal for six months before my boss had returned from her trip."

14. What is your salary range expectation?

Tip: in order to ensure that your expectations are in line with the amount they have budgeted for the position, interviewers ask this question. If you offer an extremely lower or higher salary range than the position's market value, it gives the impression you don't know your worth. Study the standard range of compensation for the indeed salaries role and aim to the higher side of your selection. Make sure the hiring manager is conscious that your rate is adjustable.

Example: "my salary expectations range from $xx, xxx to $xx, xxx, which is the average salary for an applicant with my city level of experience. Still, I'm versatile.'

How to discuss salary in a job interview

Interview question: "what are your salary expectations?"

If you are uncertain about what salary is appropriate to ask for the job to which you are applying, visit indeed's salary calculator to get a free, tailored pay range based on your venue, industry, and experience.

15. Why should we hire you?

Tip: While this question may seem like a technique of coercion, interviewees generally bring this up to give you another chance to explain why you are the best candidate. Your response will discuss the skills and experience that you are providing, and why you are suited for a good culture.

Example: "I have a passion for the production of software, which has grown stronger throughout my career. The purpose of the organization aligns with my personal values and I can already tell from my limited time in the office that this is the kind of positive culture I'd be thriving in. I want to work for an organization
that has the potential to reshape the industry and I think you're doing just that."
Visit the interview question for more on answering this question: "why should we recruit you?"
16. Do you have any questions?
Tip: this could be one of the most important questions asked during the interview process, as it allows you to discuss any subject that has not been discussed and shows the interviewer you are excited about the position. By this point, you'll probably have covered most of the basics about the job and the business already, so take the time to ask the interviewer questions about their own company experiences and obtain feedback on how you can excel if employed.
Example: "what do you love working for this enterprise? "what would this job look like success?" what are some of the usual challenges facing people in this position?
   "visit interview question for more detail on answering this question:" do you have any questions?
17. What did you like most about your previous position?

Tip: link your answer to this question to the needs of the client, and concentrate on describing your demonstrated success in your final job. Be descriptive, and set an example.

Example: "what I loved the most about my last job was the opportunity to collaboratively collaborate with other teams. Each team member was encouraged to bring in new ideas that were equally accepted by all to the project. We once worked, for example, with a client who relied on us to address a critical issue. Our team was getting together to discuss the situation. After I proposed a plan to solve the problem, we took some time to consider the pros and cons of the approach, working on how to make the concept more robust and stronger. When we put it into practice it worked better and faster than expected by everyone. The customer was very happy.'

18. What did you like most concise about your last position?

Tip: do not say anything negative about your former employer, executives, or colleagues. Make this answer about your growth in your career and your desire to join their organization.

Example: "while I loved learning and developing my time in my final job, there was a lack of opportunities in the way I wanted to advance in my career. I genuinely enjoy being challenged and getting better at what I do, which I understand is your organization's top priority for managers. That's why I'm excited to keep on thinking about this opportunity."

Just like studying for a school test, the only way to succeed is to prepare and practice in your interview. Do research on the company and the work, and practice your points of discussion until you feel confident about your answers. The more you train, the more likely you are to leave a lasting impression on fellow candidates and outperform them.

19. How do you handle stress?

Tip: this is no tricky question to see if or not you get depressed at work. Rather, how you approach a challenging moment is a measure of your problem-solving capacity. Employers want to recruit candidates who respond constructively to stress, so it's critical that your answer to that question shows personal growth.

Example: "if I concentrate on the larger picture, I can remain calm and break down my goals into smaller tasks. What is the ultimate goal that I am trying to reach? From there I make a list of items with realistic deadlines for action. Even if tomorrow's big project is due, I ask myself,' what can I do in the next 30 minutes? I've made considerable progress before I know it and that impossible dream doesn't seem so difficult.

20. What is your greatest accomplishment?

Tip: it's quick to get hooked on finding out the most impressive achievement of your single. Alternatively, consider a few achievements that show your work ethic and principles. Select cases, if you can, that also relate back to the job you are applying for. The star approach is a fantastic tool to ensure that you not only show your position but also how you have guided business results.

Example: "I have handled all of the social media content in my last job. I found other companies were playing with videos and seeing their customers engaged tremendously, And I asked my manager if we could do a study with a low budget. She agreed, so I produced an inexpensive, in-house video that doubled the interaction that we normally saw on our social channels. It has also powered conversions, with 30% of viewers visiting our website within a week of watching the video.

21. What is your teaching philosophy?

Tip: this isn't just a problem for those who apply to teaching positions. Employers might ask anyone who might lead or educate others about it. A good answer should explain what you think teaching will achieve and include specific examples to illustrate your thoughts.

Illustration: "When it comes to managing people, my teaching philosophy is to begin by asking questions which hopefully lead the person to come to a new conclusion on his own. This way, rather than feeling micro-managed, they feel control over learning. For instance, I was editing an article in my last job, written by a copywriter this I managed. There was no clear focus or hook to the story. I asked her in a one-on-one meeting what she felt was the article's main point if she had to sum it up in a sentence. From there, I asked if she felt the focus of the article was clear. She thought it wasn't clear and thought she should rework her introduction and conclusion instead. As a result, the article improved and I learned a valuable writing lesson from my direct report that she carried into her future work."

22. What does customer service mean to you?

Tip: if you ask for an open position to the public, an employer can make this request to see how you think customers should be treated. A good answer aligns with the values of the company, which you can achieve by researching your customer service policy, understanding your products and customers, and reflecting on your own customer experiences. Your answer may come from the perspective of a customer or a customer service provider.

Example: "in my experience, good customer service means taking responsibility if something goes wrong and doing what I can to solve it. For example, on a recent flight, I ordered my food only to find that they were not kept enough of my plate. Instead of just explaining the facts, the flight attendant sincerely apologized and offered me a free drink or a premium snack. For me, these excuses helped a lot to reduce things. The gift was an added bonus that made me feel valued by a client and choose the same airline for the next flight. ""

BASIC JOB SKILLS QUESTIONS

Talking about basic job skills

No matter what job you are looking for (a school principal, a store clerk, or a magazine editor), employers are looking for basic skills. Being able to demonstrate that you are reliable, organized, and able to work under pressure, among other skills, are prerequisites for any job you have to be prepared to answer these questions.

Would you say that you're reliable?

Try to understand what the interviewer really means by "reliable." if work requires staff to be punctured and planted, the researcher can mean punctual and willing to work overtime. If the job requires a high level of responsibility, the interviewer can be trusted.

Let's look at these sample answers:

Yes, I am a very reliable person. I have never been late for work in the 18 months that I worked at the Grantham plant and I am happy to work overtime if we are late as planned.

Yes, I will say that they are very reliable. My boss knows it

I'm the kind of person who can let me do an important mission and don't forget me or leave me until I'm done.

What's your absenteeism/sickness record like?

Employers are genuinely concerned that their workers are late for work or are on sick days. I hope you can explain your concerns by saying: I have a good history of absenteeism, I've only had x days off in the last few years. The key is that "x" is less than a little.

If you took a few days off, make sure you give a convincing reason. But continue to emphasize that the reason is gone now. For instance:

I still had to be out of work for four weeks, so I broke a ligament when I ran over a pot in the workshop. But now I'm fully recovered and I have a clean health status, so it won't be a problem in the future.

Never put in your sickness file, as employers frequently check. Job offers are often presented as a reference (check your work history with previous employers) and a lie in this phase can lead employers to give up your job.

How would you define your time management skills?

For most jobs, employers are finding time management skills: the ability to distinguish between what needs to be done now and what can be expected. Of course, you have to say that you have good time management skills.

A great tactic is to say that you always prioritize the most important and urgent tasks at the top of the stack. When this doesn't work, let's say you ask your colleagues for help or check if the term can be moved. As a last resort, you can say that you just have to work and be late to do everything.

Continue to demonstrate your time management skills by setting an example of when you had a priority between different tasks.

For example, last week, I had a client who wanted an emergency order to be processed immediately while my boss needed some financial details. There was no means she could do both, so I asked a staff member to process the client's order while gathering the data my boss needed.

Talking about yourself

Time management is ultimately the ability to distinguish urgency and importance. Emergency describes whether a task should be completed very quickly or if it can wait a few hours or a few weeks. The importance describes the extent to which the function should be performed: some functions are absolutely essential, while others may be less crucial.

Are you an organized person?

Of course, you are very organized! Illustrate your organizational skills by talking about some of the methods or systems you use to organize your work, such as:

Make lists to do

Keep files and memories in various projects develop a routine or process

Use Gantt tables, spreadsheets, computer programs, or even charts (but don't speak unless you really use them) to track the progress of various tasks

Remember to show that you are really organized by giving a brief example of a project that you have organized or coordinated.

Be careful not to say that it is so organized that it would be difficult for you to function without your working methods and methods. Sometimes, the world of work poses unforeseen problems and situations that you only have to solve spontaneously.

Alternatively, a researcher may ask: how far is your office working? Such a request means that the interviewer probably believes that an orderly desk is a sign of an orderly mind, so a complete qualification goes to candidates who can describe an orderly workspace.

Do you work well under pressure?

Although the answer to this question is obviously yes, be careful not to overdo it as long as you can face the pressure. Try to relate your answer to the questions that the job may require.

For example, if the job may be causing significant pressure, the following response may be quite adequate:

Prospectus on pressure. My worst night is a completely predictable and mundane job. I really appreciate the fact that my work is different every day and that you never know what new situations or difficulties you are facing.

If the job is going well, saying that you enjoy working under pressure can raise questions in the mind of a researcher about the boredom of your job. So try and answer in the line of:

I may face occasional discoveries of having to work under pressure; for example, during the last two days of each month, he always gets a little frantic. But for the most part, I appreciate the fact that it's a job I can really learn and understand in detail and be good at.

If you need to demonstrate beyond any doubt that you are different from pressure, use the acronym car to provide an example. Make sure the result at the end of your story is positive!

Would you say that you're creative?

An interviewer can ask if you are creative or innovative, and for all practical purposes, you can treat it as the same question. Your answer to this question relies on the nature of the job for which you are interviewed. If you are applying for a job that requires high levels of artistic ability and visual creativity (such as a graphic designer or advertising director), say yes and prepare a portfolio with at least some examples of how creative you are.

Keep in mind that employers are looking for not just creative ideas, but real products, tangibles, designs, and inventions. So, make sure your examples describe how an idea came to your head in a solution that benefited your team or organization.

If you do not ask for a job that requires a high level of creativity and you believe that creativity is not really one of your strengths, this is an opportunity where you have to feel comfortable, to be honest. But it continues to highlight some of your key strengths and qualities

If work is administrative, you can get away with saying that creativity is not one of your main assets. I have heard from many managers who dislike interviewers saying that, although creativity is not one of their main strengths, they try to create an atmosphere in their teams that promotes creativity through breastfeeding, organization. Of workshops and outdoor days. , and supporting the ideas that team members have.

Would you say you're good with detail?

For most questions, the answer to this question should be yes. Of course, employers do not want to induce people into underwear.

If the job requires very detailed work, give a simple example of how to ensure that your work is of constant quality:

In my work, it is very important to get all the correct numbers, so I always check the data after entering. And I am happy to say that during my two years of work so far, no one has found a mistake in my calculations.

The exceptions to this general rule are managers. For middle managers, employers often expect to pay attention to the big picture instead of getting tired of the details. So, if you already manage a large average team, say at least a dozen or more people, then you can catch up with it:

I must admit that details are not one of my strengths. Try to stay focused on the great picture. However, I am always sure that I have good people on my team who can handle the details.

How do you respond to change?

Researchers do not want to end up employing an inflexible and inappropriate job. I'm sure you know the tip: the grumpy person who complains about how things are "these days" and constantly remembers "good old days" before this or that change.

The world of work is changing swiftly, with factors at stake such as globalization, mergers and acquisitions, the change agenda, and efficiency efforts. Talking about how to deal with one of these changes illustrates your ability to deal with the change.

Make sure you can show that you are ready to adapt to new circumstances, perhaps along the lines of:

Some people left our team in the space of a week, which means we had little staff for over a month. The rest of the team had to readjust our shifts to make sure the help desk was still busy. We volunteered for some additional changes because we knew our customers would not have to rely on others to handle their problems.

Another tactic that shows that you are not only facing change but that you are excellent, is explaining how you have helped others to overcome change. Maybe you had colleagues who weren't sure about a new wheel, but you talked about it. Or you have agreed to work as part of a project team, committee, or task force responsible for part of the change process. Some of these examples show that not only can you respond to change reactively, but you can also contribute proactively.

How are you with new technology?

A variation on the issue of their ability to cope with change, this demand for technology tends to be more demanding for older candidates. If you don't think so, new technologies are being introduced all the time, from new computers and laptops to cell phones and electronic cards. Concerned employers do not want to employ people who have difficulty mastering the principles of their use.

Give as concrete an example as possible to familiarize yourself with a new face of the technology that has been introduced in your work:

We used transparent acetates and antique-style aerial projectors to teach seminars. But the university chose to introduce laptops and projectors and asked us all to prepare our PowerPoint documents. I am happy to say that after attending information sessions on the use of new technologies, I have become a true fan of this new way of working.

What software packages are you familiar with?

If you opt for a role where software packages are important, it is usually a good idea to include them somewhere in your resume. If an employer asks about your level of proficiency with different packages, be sure to give examples of their exploits. For instance:

I am responsible for creating the monthly department newsletter, which usually means using this package to format tabs and contributions from others. I also need to import the images and create detailed proposal documents for my manager. And I can merge contact lists with letter templates to create marketing emails.

In general, even the most experienced managers should be aware of the use of a computer. Partnerships with major law firms and city leaders with budgets of hundreds of millions of pounds must read and send their own emails and write some words in a document. So, if you can't do at least these two Fundamental tasks, make sure you find someone to teach you how to do them!

Seek preparation, or have a relative or friend show you how to use the basics of the Microsoft office kit if you really don't know anything about computers. Microsoft is by far the workplace's most popular software developer, which makes good software.

How would you rate yourself as . . .?

An interviewer may ask you to evaluate yourself according to a number of criteria, such as your skills as a leader, a team player, a teacher, or a researcher. Obviously, you have to start by saying that you are a good leader, a team player, or whatever. Don't let it stop you from selling yourself, you can bet that other candidates make all kinds of outlandish claims about their quality.

To support your statement, continue to tell a short anecdote or cite an example to explain why you think you are rated so high. If you've won awards or received praise or positive feedback from colleagues or clients, this may be the time to remember.

If an interviewer asks for a numerical rating, avoid giving it a 10/10 rating. Trying to pretend perfectly you seem incredibly tired. A score of 8/10 is more reasonable. Continuing something like: I think I'm very good at x, but there's always more to learn. This answer shows a suggestion of humility and a desire to improve even more: good job opportunities.

How do your skills and experience fit?

Tell us about tea and your latest works. Whatever you do to answer this question, do not start with "I was born and raised ..." the interviewing authority is trying to find out exactly what he has done professionally to evaluate his ability to do this job. He or she does not care where you were born or raised.

What sort of job are you looking for? In other words, "what I'm looking for is the same thing I'm looking for?" if you have done your new research, you know exactly what type of position you are looking for. Otherwise, the answer is: "I am looking for a position that will help me improve a business and challenge myself based on my experience and my background."

Describe in detail your last two positions. Even if you have done your presentation well in the last two or three jobs you have done (what you did, how you did it, what you did for it to be successful), you may still receive this request. Basically, it gives exactly the same description you gave in your professional career and experience, but maybe with a little more detail. Be sure to precede your answer to this question with "I really like this job" or "I really like the job I do," explaining in detail what you do. Ask the question: "Was I clear?" it may "look like a job" but being fired, reduced, fired, not making enough money, not being promoted, etc. There are many reasons to change jobs, even if people like what they do. In fact, any derogatory comment on a current or previous job may reduce the chances of being insured.

Leave me a day at your current or most recent job. If you made your presentation correctly at the beginning, the interviewing authority will not ask you to do so. If so, make sure you have concise answers from 60 to 90 seconds. Highlight the parts of the job that are closer to the ones you are interviewing. Just make sure you apply this answer. It is surprising how many times candidates have answered this question, simply because they have not been trained.

What was the hardest part about your last two jobs? Whatever your answer, you have to say, "even though it was the hardest part of the job, I have always been up to the challenge." then, communicate in highly appreciated and optimistic tones about the most difficult part of the job. You could also add something like "accomplishing this difficult part of the job has made me a better person." share a short story on how to overcome a difficult challenge in each of your latest assignments.

What do you want in a job? Obviously, you have to answer this question with an answer that has something to do with the job or position you require. Make sure you say something like "I like the challenge of learning in almost every job I have" and also, "I'm looking for a position that helps me improve a business and challenge me"

What do you want in a job? Whenever you have a question like this, stay away from mere low-level incentives at work. Answers like "hey, I'm looking for more money in a job" won't get you far. You always want to highlight a higher level of thinking by emphasizing the concepts of

Growth and satisfaction. Something like "well, I won't work to be difficult. I like to challenge myself every day. Being challenged will grow personally and professionally, and I find that if you grow personally and professionally, the economy, benefits, and many other things like 'and they still take care of themselves "good answer.

Write down the best work you've ever had and why it was so much better than the others you've had. Regardless of what you describe, be similar to the position for which you are currently interviewing. Something like, "you know, there have been wonderful aspects to almost every job I've had. I really like them all, and they are all 'better' for different reasons" is an excellent way to precede the answer.

How do you define success? Simple answer: "when you contribute to the success of an organization, you succeed. We both grow. Well, you can tell a story about the 'success' you've had in your last two or two jobs. Remember, people love stories. And remember long after that they remember almost everything else.

What is your biggest accomplishment in each of your last three jobs? Make sure you tell a story about each success you have achieved in each job. Whatever attribute is associated with the result, it must be backed up by a short and interesting story. It's an easy question to prepare for the answers, and you'll be asked about all the people you talk to, so be prepared.

I'm creating just call one or two cases where you've been creative and tell the story. Keep all stories short and to the point.

What do you know about the position you require? How little do you know about the position you can express. And if you don't know much about it, be sure to add a request at the end of what you know, something like "can you clarify what you think publishing means?" this may be part of a catch-22 request. A smart-aleck, and you'll meet some, can come back and say, "well, if you don't know much about what you're asking, how do you know you can do it?" and the answer to any smart question like this is: "I know your organization is the type I want to join, and from what I understand, my skills best match this job." can you clarify what exactly this position requires? "

How do we know you have been successful in this job? Now that's a good question. Whenever you are asked to preach the future, explain that you have succeeded in everything you have done in the past and that there is no reason to believe that you will not be so successful in this work. . This kind of "predicting the future" question is often asked. Remember that the alternative answer is: "I'm already successful; that's why it will happen again. And if you have to support that claim, you can do it with success stories."

What is the most recent business lesson you learned and how did you learn it? You have to communicate that you have learned life and demonstrate what you have just learned and how. Tell a story

What have you learned in particular from the jobs you have had lately? This is about a skill or lesson you have learned. Tangible attributes such as persistence, determination, respect, loyalty, etc. They are excellent at highlighting. Short stories and effective stories.

What made you want to become a _____? It doesn't matter what you hit a blank. You might be able to say that you have always had an enchantment or passion for certain aspects of your profession. For example, if it's a sales position, you want to talk about the passion for communicating ideas, helping people solve their problems, and so on. If it is a position that requires mathematical skills like accounting, engineering, etc., you want to communicate that you have always had a passion and love for numbers, science and making things work, etc. Maybe you had a mentor, a father, a teacher, etc., who trained the type of profession in which you are involved. Whatever you do, do not communicate that you "stumble" in your profession, he "chose you", you could find nothing better to do, or you thought he was as good as anyone else. Profession anything that communicates a lack of direction, passion, or involuntary career decisions will not work.

What can you contribute most to our organization? Simple answer: "in addition to my excellent professional performance, as I mentioned in previous posts, I work harder and have more commitment to work than most employees. My relationship with God and my family comes from my job. There is nothing better than this answer. If you have communicated well in the presentation portion of the interview, it will only reinforce what you have done in the past.

What do you know about our business? What is the biggest challenge or problem for our business? What trends do you see in our profession or industry? What do you know about our competitors? What do you know about our society? These are all questions to which you should find the answers in your search on the company and company you are. Even if you do not get the right answers, when you show that you have done a thorough investigation of the organization and company that you are, it will respond well to the question. Most interviewing authorities do not really hope to know their business too closely but want to see if you have made an effort to get to know them both and their business.

What would be your ideal working group? How do you define a "suitable" work environment? Do you work well with other people? Do you fancy working alone or with other people? Do you need and appreciate a lot of surveillance? Do you work best with large groups or small groups? The answer to questions like these (at work alone or with other people, in large or small groups, etc.) Should be answered with something like: "well, I was lucky to be able to work at all." different types of environments. I have worked well alone., with others, in relaxed work environments, in stressful work environments, in large groups, and in small groups. I think, fortunately, they are adaptable and work. Good in almost any environment. If the maintenance authority wants specific examples of any of these conditions, make sure you have one or two different job histories to prove your point.

Why did you ask for our society? This is an opportunity to demonstrate the research you have done in business and to communicate how your individual skills, experience, or background can be contributed. Try to be as definite as you can about what you've learned about the company, and how it can help.

I don't think that with your experience and your experience, you can do this job. What do you think? Unless it is a relatively strange situation, it is unlikely that you will even interview this person if you cannot get the job done. It's more of a test to see how you respond instead of exactly what you say. But something else: "the people I worked within the last two jobs thought I was disqualified before enrolling. But I did very well in both. I'm a super performer and I'm still able to overcome my apparent skills." then tell a story, if applicable.

Why do you have to hire me? "because I can do the job, I work a lot, people like me are not at great risk and we can come to a conclusion about money."

Why weren't you promoted early? If you are so talented, why haven't you been promoted? Do not leave a request as "under your skin". You can never let a question like this stop you, and it's best not to show any irritation. Just to say that in the organizations where you were, there was a "neck" of very busy people available for the few emerging promotions. While you know that the quality of your work deserves to be promised, the likelihood was highly unlikely just because there were too many people looking for promotions that were in the business longer than you. That is actually one of the reasons you expect to change jobs.

How does our position compare to the other opportunities you are interviewing? Be honest and quite brief. It is always a good plan to inform a searcher what other organizations are considering.

If you feel comfortable saying what your organizations are, be fine. Always be sure to say something like, "given everything I know about the other opportunities I've interviewed, working here with you seems to be a little better." just make sure you have good reasons to say so.

You don't really have as much experience as we want; why should we engage you? Answering a question like this is simple. "you know, it's very interesting, and for every job I've had, I've never been able to work with all the experience my former employers wanted. In fact, I entered three of them where I was simply assured because I had more." as you can see, I've succeeded in all the positions I've held, even though I haven't had the experience before I start, some people understand things faster than others and realize who I am blessed in that way. And I've come to learn things that I don't necessarily have experience with and that they do extremely well. "

Have you ever "failed" in a job? Answer this question with a "focus light". Say something like, "well, I'm like a ballplayer who never lost, just ran out of time." even the few things I think of and that others might think of as "failures", I actually see them as an adversary. Like most people, everything I didn't go as I would have liked. But even when he didn't, I learned from it. ""

If I could, what would change in the position for which the interview is? You can start the application here simply with something like: "based on almost everything I know, it seems that what you ask in the job function is right. You don't really know the position well enough to know what you could. Or be changed. ""

What do you love most about this position? And who do you like least about this post? Be prepared to address a particular aspect of the job that will be a positive challenge for you. The answer is something like: "I can't wait to take responsibility for this job. (this) and (that) jobs are very stimulating. A well-experienced manager will give me the opportunity to develop what I have. Learned. I think there's nothing about the job I've heard so far that I don't like. I'm sure there will be things I like more than others, but that's normal in every job. "

Do you fancy to delegate or be a "practical" employee? Simple answer: "I feel comfortable delegating the things that need to be delegated and personally doing the things I do best. I know that even when the job is delegated, not everyone does the job exactly as I should. But I feel comfortable with that."

If you can start your career again, what else would you do?

? Please answer this question carefully. If you answer this question in the negative, it will shoot in the foot. Being derogatory to say something like "well, I prefer to be a professional golfer" won't take you long. Instead, communicate that you have made mistakes in your career, but that these are minor mistakes, that you have learned from them, and, looking back, there is nothing in the general sense that you have done much differently.

If you could choose one organization to work for, who would you go to? This can be a trick question. He says enthusiastically with a big smile on his face: "without a doubt, this company is usually what I want to work for," doesn't seem authentic. Then it might say something like, "all the organizations I talk to are quality companies with like-minded people. All the positions I've interviewed have their strengths and weaknesses. A job is more or less what do once you show up and start working. I consider the opportunity to work here at your company as one of the best opportunities available to me. "

What is the latest skill you have learned? Try to maintain the answer to a business task. Learning to skate or play golf can really motivate you, but most of the hiring authorities aren't interested in getting to know you. Talk about one of the business skills you recently learned or the business seminar you attended. Tell a story

How do you keep information and professional? It's like a question: "what professional books have you read?" you better have a very good answer. Being a member of a professional company helps. A mere subscription to professional newspapers is not a good answer. You may have this question quite frequently, but once you have an answer, you can give it to everyone.

What is the most important job lesson you learned from the jobs you had? Choose one or two important "lessons" you've learned from each job you've done and relate it briefly.

Do you want to go to management? This can be a loaded request. If you have not interviewed for a management position and answer that you would like to join management, it could be eliminated. The recruiting authority may feel that since you are not committed to a management position and you do not know if a managerial position will materialize, you will leave as soon as you find out that the address is not available. On the other hand, if you say something like, "well, I never considered a management position," it might not be ambitious. So the answer is something like, "I think I have a chance to manage it, but I know that the" good "leaders" are also good "Indians." if it shows me that I am in any role, if there are opportunities for progress, I am sure I will be considered.

I interact to do this job well. If you do the work, tomorrow and the positions ahead will take care of them. ""

Have you ever had fire from someone? Describe the circumstances? The answer to this question must be made emotionally and empathetically. If you answer the question in an authoritative and dominant way, "the sobs deserve it," you will not be respected. A sure but empathetic answer in the sense of: "shooting is one of the most difficult tasks for a manager. But I have found that if done in a very careful, well-documented, reasoned, and business way, even if the discomfort on both sides, can be done with great grace. Then, I could add a brief history of a circumstance in which I had to shoot someone. After all, he must communicate that he was unfortunate, but that he should do it and he did a lot of grace.

What kind of people have you engaged with and what are you looking for in these people? If you have been involved in the hiring process, you will want to describe the type of people you have hired. You want to make sure you establish a rational business approach and reason to employ someone. Discover a process and a description of your success.

Describe an important project you have worked on and how you have contributed to the overall good of your employer. If you have been involved in an important project, just be prepared to describe the project in detail. Describe your role, how you interact with each other's roles, and how the project succeeded.

Have you ever been involved in long-term planning? If so, simply explain how you got involved. Do not pretend that you have been involved in long-term planning, if you are right, because you may be asked about your contribution, and your credibility will be questioned if you cannot talk about what you have done.

What percentage of your week or month have you spent on different work duties? You will not receive this request very often, but it does not hurt to get a concept of the percentage of time spent on all your work activities. If you respond to this general statement as "I did it until it's done," you don't seem to be a disciplined person.

Can you work hours on weekends or hours? On the one hand, you have to be the guy who does everything he does to get the job done. On the other hand, you do not want to be the type of employee you have to work nights and weekends just to get all the work done to a minimum. So the answer to this question is, "I will do whatever it takes to get the job done." over the course of my career, I have found that since I am a hard worker, focus on the task at hand and not waste time with unproductive cohorts, therefore, I do more work in much less time than most. I work at noon and on weekends if needed, but this has not been needed in the past. ""

How long do you think it will require to make a significant contribution to our organization? It's a slightly loaded question. If you "guess" for too long, you're not sure, and if you "earn" a shorter period of reality, then you look stupid. So the best answer should be something like, "in my current job, I started making a significant contribution almost immediately. The nature of the work was such that I was able to get in and out and have an immediate impact. It was very first, because of the nature of the company's activities it took five or six months to make a significant impact. Everyone I've worked with has always said that doing a quick study and doing things very quickly is difficult. To speculate the speed at which I can. Make a significant contribution until you find a job and become familiar with it. However, I can guarantee you that I will run as quickly as possible. I realize that I or someone else is assured to contribute as soon as possible.

How many hours in your previous assignments did you have to work each week to get the job done? Don't fall prey to this loaded request. Your answer should be something like "gee whiz, I'm not a guard. I really don't." if you have a job where you are paid overtime, the hiring authority may be concerned about having to pay several overtime hours. Then, in such a situation, I respond by saying, "I always take great care to make sure I don't have to work out of time if I don't." I work very fast and usually do my job on time. Of course, my references corroborate this. If he feels that overtime is not a problem, he says, "I work very efficiently. I did everything I required to do the job on time, with high quality. Whenever I needed it, it's time I needed. . "

You do not have much experience in some aspects of this work. How do we know if you can actually do it? The answer should be something like, "looking back on most of the jobs I've had, I didn't really have the experience that my previous employers wanted. The interview process here was where people were ready to help, so she was absolutely certain that she would have no problem doing all aspects of the job.

What were the things you didn't like about your last job? Answer this question with things that do not have anything to do with your show or skills. Something like, "well, I got frustrated because most people were very negative about the bad situation in the business. The company was finally sold; unfortunately, almost everyone had a negative attitude. Or something like: "well, when work slows down when crawling, our main distributor has stopped buying. Instead of looking for things to do and thinking about what we can do to improve the business, most of the company's employees have complained. Some of us have encountered and found alternatives. Everything you "don't like", doing something of value or something you can't do anything about.

What reservations could you have working here? The answer is simple: "no one knows. No business or business is perfect, and I'm sure it has all its positives and negatives like any other business."

How many levels of administration have you had to communicate? Be honest, knowing that the purpose of this question is to discern how many levels above you feel comfortable with. If you are only communicating with one or two previous levels, you need to ensure that they communicate that it was more linked to your job function than your inability to communicate with the senior management.

In your opinion, what makes the job that you interview different from the jobs you had or other jobs for which you interviewed? Prepare for this application and consider the unique aspects of the particular job for which you are interviewing. Be sure to communicate some very positive reasons why the job for which you were interviewed would be "better suited" than you have had in the past.

Are you a good employee / manager / engineer / accountant / salesperson / administrative support person / etc? How do you know? This very simple question requires a very simple answer: "I really like what they do. I'm very good at receiving so many positive answers for the work they do. My performance appraisals and salary evaluations have always been excellent."

How did your current job prepare you to take on more responsibility? It's best to have an answer to this question before you ever ask. You want to emphasize that there are certain aspects of your work that go beyond personal and professional. Remember to make sure you "like" your job, but you're ready for a new challenge. Emphasizing that he has grown as much as possible in his current position and can cite one or two stories about how he could have contributed more, but it was simply not necessary because there are many people who did all this during the process. The interview. You may be able to communicate that you have one or two or even three skills and abilities available at work. In this way, he always communicates: "I can contribute more and I am not limited." it relates to your personal "growth" rather than a personal "problem."

Can you move now or in the future? The answer to any relocation request, now or in the future, should always be: "I will surely do what my business and my career serve." the amendment would be included. ""

In what areas could your boss do better? Indeed, there is only one way to answer this question: "I have respect for my current boss. He does his job very well. There may be things he can do a little better, but they will certainly be less."

How long do you think your boss has evaluated your performance? "all the supervisors or leaders I've done a good job evaluating my performance."

How did your leader or his previous leaders do? This is a slightly wrong question. We both see how we react and find the answer. Prepare yourself for a question like this and understand that the simple answer is: "tell me exactly what the goals are and leave me alone."

Do you have financial responsibility? What was your budget? Having trouble meeting your budget? Be ready to answer any type of questions you may have about your budget responsibility.

Give me an example of your previous work experience that demonstrates your ability to develop action plans or create programs that support strategic goals and leadership. You have to have three or four stories that can be used interchangeably with questions like this. If in a previous answer, you told a story that could be an answer to that question, you would not want to tell the same story. In fact, candidates tend, if not well disposed of, to tell the same story or two more than they should. Most questions a story could answer are similar. If you continue to answer different questions with the same two stories, you will seem superficial. So be prepared with a series of different stories that can respond to different situations.

Tell us about an experience that illustrates your preference for being proactive in talking and keeping in touch with others or waiting for others to speak first or communicate with you. Again, as mentioned above, it's best to have a positive story to tell. If you have to think or meditate on the answer, it does not seem decisive.

Do you know when to drive and when to follow? Examples of both should be given. You have to prepare them for these kinds of questions. Again, if you have to think or think, you seem to not know what you are doing. The situations in which you guide and where you follow are appropriate.

Can you identify critical needs in one situation and put others on hold? The answer is "of course." and one or two stories in which you need to identify critical situations will work.

If this post has been offered, how long will it take us to make the decision? "if they offered me the job, I could be informed during the day, up to two."

BEHAVIORAL INTERVIEW QUESTIONS

Behavioral interview questions and answers
The interviewer can ask questions for typical interview questions which will ultimately show your educational background, skills, skills, etc. But the interviewer focuses on how you have been able to deal with different work situations in the past in the conduct interview questions. Your response represents your talents, your abilities, and your personality.

Give me an example of a significant target you set in the past and tell me about your progress in achieving it

Most interviewers are asking the question because they want to know how you achieved and the issues that helped you achieve success at that particular time.

Using the star method is advisable to help you get a more organized response.

Using this method, you'll get all the details the interviewer is looking for.

The star technique includes the following steps:

Situation: you should begin by defining the situation you were in or the mission you needed to accomplish. You have to identify a given circumstance or event.

Task: describe the aim you anticipated to accomplish

Action: describe the specific action you have taken to address the situation. You clarify the steps you have taken to achieve your goals, too.

Result: you must be able to give specific details of the outcome of your actions. The outcome will be an important part of your response because the interviewer asked you about a time you've been productive. That is, there probably would be an impact.

To answer this question you must:

Verify that the situation you describe is true

Make sure you are plain and realistic

Sample answers

"I also set a personal target in my current internship program to accomplish my aim for my internship which is improving my it supports knowledge. I have set a goal before my internship program finishes to learn the basics of computer programming. I also worked closely with it and the programming team to ensure that I learned my skills. I had1-year experience in supporting it at the end of my internship and was able to develop my programming skills to an intermediate level."

"I set out to improve my customer-service skills from moderate to progress this year. I wanted to work closely with the customer service team and learn from the experts about the nature of customer service. I've also taken specialized customer service, training classes. After working closely with the customer service department for this, I was amazed at how good I was with my customer service skills that even customers spoke to my boss very well about me."

Describe times when you were not very happy or satisfied with yours

Performance

When interviewers ask this question, they want to really understand how you are doing your job (how much you care about your work) and to what degree you feel responsible for the success of your position.

Until you attempt the question take note of the following:

Make sure the illustration you are giving is important to the job that you are applying for

Talk about your prior role

Give concrete reasons why you don't feel satisfied

Provide an example of what you learned

State how your lessons helped you develop

Sample answers

"I was disappointed with what I was meant to do when I got my first job as a marketer and got a month goal, so I just went out to get customers the way I thought I should. I found at the end of the month that I was the only one within the team that didn't achieve the target. I felt pretty bad.

I spoke about it to my boss, then he told me to be more cautious and to create a plan before doing any action. Working with his guidance, I devised a marketing strategy and broke down plans before I left. I become one of the lead marketers in my business, after working with my strategy. I found that planning is very necessary and that doing too many things does not guarantee success at the same time.

"at one point in my current job, I realized I used to work in a team and that's why I became too dependent on other team members to do stuff. My supervisor spoke to me about that, and I started to be more accountable in carrying out my role and I wanted to start working more independently. I worked closely with my supervisor to allow her to give me her personal tasks. I develop a better sense of independence in carrying out my task, after doing more tasks alone. After I began to work independently, I gained other skills such as advanced excel skills that I applied to improve my work."

Tell me about a time when you worked under close supervision or supervision which was extremely loose. (how did you cope with this?)

Most of the time interviewers ask this question, they want to learn how well you can function in a team, how you can contribute to a boss, and how well you can work independently.

Speak always about when answering the question;

How you finally handled the situation

What you learned

The action you took to handle the circumstance

What the situation was like

Sample answers

"I was working under a boss in my former job, who was almost always busy with official duties, and he didn't really have the time to supervise my task. As an entry-level member of staff with very little human resources experience it was very difficult for me. I wanted to ask my colleagues in the same department how they were doing their job and they've always been able to support me with my task. Gaining more information from others made me work easier and brought my supervisor results with ease." (working under loose surveillance)

"I worked as a web creator for our media team in my previous job but the supervision of my line manager was too direct and almost constant. She watched all that I do and sat almost all day by me. I felt very uncomfortable with it because it almost always put me under pressure. I found over time that she didn't trust me to handle projects alone because I was new. I decided I'd build her confidence for the projects that I'd handled. She agreed reluctantly, I talked to her about handling a project without supervision. I've done my best to research the project and to perform well. The project was very successful, and since then she didn't really need to monitor me so intensively." (working under close surveillance).

Inform me about a time when you went beyond your duty to do a job

If interviewers ask this question, they just want to know how serious about your work you are. They'd just love to know how far you can go in getting your job done. It is also used by interviewees to learn how results focused you are.

Often interviewers ask this question to see if you are the kind of person who is willing to take up challenges and goes beyond the norm to make sure the job is done properly (if necessary)

These are the aspects on which you should concentrate when answering the question:

Concentrate on the target of the question that is beyond

Emphasis on attributes and not circumstances

Concentrate on knowing what the interviewer means beyond your obligations

Understand how you'd explain to the interviewer about your duty.

Stay away from the following:

Stay away from exaggerating anything

Don't be too fast to answer the question

Stop giving an illustration that is not related to the question

Sample answers

"for me, I think going beyond my job call is making sure the right things are done at the right time and not just doing what I'm supposed to be doing. A very large corporation has been calling us to get them the invoice for a product range. The mail was delivered to our mailbox. Luckily, I picked it up from the mailbox and noticed it would be late by Monday and it was Friday already. I took the mail home to do my work and sent the invoice to them even though it was not my task. They were given the multi-million deal the next week.

"it's going beyond my call of duty to make sure that everything works out well. I once served as a logistics manager, for example, and one day our big customer made an order that needs to leave that night, I decided to join people doing the package even if I was a manger until nearly midnight. I didn't want the customer to lose confidence in our dream that reflects national distribution. I figured that was the only thing I could do for the moment to save.

Tell me about a time you disagreed with a decision that was made at work

Employers recognize that no two people are the same, and there will be points of consensus and disagreement when working with people there. Interviewers also ask this question because they want to learn how well you can function in a team, and how well you can manage conflict.

When answering this question, you should focus on:
The alternative suggestion that you offered
The decision you disagreed with
The result of the disagreement

Why you disagreed with the decisions

You should avoid:

Use of negative words about people who are involved in decision making

Be careful to not sound opinionated

Avoid being defensive

Sample answers

"my team members were working on a company report, and my boss and other team members were intent on setting time deadlines to help us make the release. I dissented with that, I know setting a time deadline would put you on your feet to get the job done, but it also creates a stressful atmosphere and members of the team will work under duress that won't help them see things from their creative space. I told them it's best for us to take our time and come up with something that's worth it in the end. My boss and other team members agreed with me after a lot of deliberations and the report nevertheless stood out as one of the best we've ever achieved.

"I was working on a project that so many people needed us to reach out to. My manager had told me to go out to rallies so we can build our plan conscious. I did not agree with his order to go to a rally on Lagos street. I advised him we would run an internet campaign to make it quicker, simpler, and cheaper. He was very impressed with the suggestion I made with my online campaign and we were able to reach out to the number of people we wanted to reach."

Give me an example of a significant target you set in the past and tell me about your progress in achieving it

Interviewers are asking this question because they want to get an understanding of how committed you are, how purposeful you are, and also want to get an idea of your dream and mission to see how it leads to you being the right fit for the job.

Use the star approach to effectively answer that question

You should focus on the following:

You should focus on telling the interviewer the goal

How to reach the goal?

The action you have taken to succeed

The result of the action you have taken.

Sample answers

"When I first got to my present company, I realized that the essence of what the company wants to achieve is to improve the customer base. I set the target of adding at least 10 percent to the company's existing customer base. To do that, I studied what tool the company uses, and decided to take a marketing and sales promotion course. I was able to make better use of both the online marketing strategy and offline and pr at the end of the course. I was able to contribute over 10 percent to our customer base at the end of that year and my boss was very happy

"in my previous company, during my internship, I set a goal for me to develop my human resources career even though I was just a front desk officer. I have always spoken and worked with the department of human resources to get a taste of what they do. I have taken an hr course and studied indirectly in my company. I was able to find my career path at the conclusion of my one-year internship program and gained useful human resources experience."

Could you give an example of a time you enjoyed your job (what happened, what was your reaction)

If an interviewer asks you this question, the interviewer may only want to understand what you mean by success. Simply put; the interviewer needs to get an understanding of your concept of success, and a sense of what makes you feel satisfied. The interviewer also desires to know how much of a concern you have about the company's growth.

When answering this question, focus on:

Why you were pleased with the actions

What exactly you did

What effect did the action have

The steps you took that led to success

Avoid:

Exaggeration

Bragging

Sample answers

"I was doing a topic that would inspire people to do a blog post. So I've done research on topics that will interest people and a subject that can help people get better. I asked a few friends for their feedback and I began the post. I also attained out to CEOs that could help us. When we published the story, we realized that we got much more exposure than we initially planned and we received a huge result from testimonials that affected our revenues that year. I was very pleased with the path I took to make a success of this project.

"I worked as a sales intern in my first job but I was really interested in pushing my selling capabilities to the next stage. I told my boss that I should be allowed to sell a product myself without any help or assistance. She agreed, so I've done my research, using my internet and skills to sell more than 90 percent of the product I received. I was really happy that I was able to achieve this success even with my limited internship access."

Can you give an illustration of a time that you solved a problem?

If interviewers ask this question they really are interested in how to solve a problem. The interviewer looks forward to learning your problem-solving skills in order to learn how well you will manage on-the-job challenges.

How to answer this question:

Explain clearly the method you used to solve the problem.

Identify the problem

Why did you decide to use the approach?

What was the solution to the problem?

Sample answers

"in my position as the growth leader in my previous company, I've been in charge of managing the company's growth and ensuring that everything that will eventually lead to increased sales works well. I found at one point that our growth was restricted to just one source (online source) and this limited the revenue potential we would have accumulated over time.

Our offline activities have been declining rapidly, and according to my study, I have found that a better portion of our sales within our niche can best be accessed from offline activities. And I called our sales and marketing department to speak to them to see how best we should handle the situation. We agreed and came up with a lot of offline branding and pr tactics to put our brand before people's eyes. After a while, we noticed we had a good number of walk-in requests now and this also improved our customer base and revenue

"I was responsible for personnel health and management in my role as a human resources manager. During the course of my job, I found that it was difficult for us to get the best candidates for our and company roles. This became a big issue because this was the service we provide to consumers and it would have an impact on our credibility not getting it right.

I called a meeting with other executives in human resource and we tried to find out what we're not doing well, and how easily we can get customers applicants as soon as possible. After a series of deliberations, we found that we are not looking the right way for our candidates, so we decided to add a link to our website where we can have a candidates ' database for different positions. We have also decided to search for candidates using online tools like Linkedin. We found out that we're waiting until there's so much pressure to start headhunting for talent, so we decided to start processing the applicant request as soon as an application is made. All the reformation helped us to quickly get candidates and also kept our customers.

Can you give an illustration of a time when you had work difficulties?

This is a wide-ranging problem and may come in different types. For these reasons, interviewees are actually asking this question; they want to understand what you find difficult (this depends largely on how you choose to answer the question). To know how to identify a problem, and how to fix it.

If you answer that question you will focus on the following:

Reflect on thinking about a difficult situation to a question you have solved successfully

Concentrate on learning about an issue related to your job

Inform the interviewer carefully on what caused the problem

State what actions you have taken that solved the problems

The star technique will assist you to answer this question well

You should also don't make the following mistakes:

Try not to talk about your personal problem

Avoid focusing too much on the damage caused by the problem, concentrate more on what you have learned.

sample answers

"in my current internship in the department of product management, the customer service staff sent me a customer who was really unhappy with our product's unique features. The customer explained that this was the main reason she purchased the product and she's so angry that the product can't meet their needs. I talked to everybody in the team to see how the issue can be solved, but the solution wasn't coming.

So I talked with the customer and told her I'll make sure we send her a new one with the features she wants to see. So rather than just solving the problem, I decided to add the function to our new product and to advertise the product when it is out with the new function.

At the end of the day, we tried to solve the woman's issue as well as please our customers by adding a purpose to our goods. This led to a great understanding of the brand and the company.'

"in my current position as executive of customer satisfaction, we found we focused on getting more customers to buy our product and services than keeping them. This was a major problem that had yet to be overcome by all in the business. This created a lot of friction for the marketing team, as they wanted to think about getting customers.

I was talking about how we could boost our customer retention so we could create trust in our customers. I've come up with a plan for us to improve our customer reward system and also how we can boost our customer engagement. I decided we would build social media pages on various platforms where we can reach out and support our customers even before they visit our website. So we have strengthened engagement with our customers and thus we have been able to increase our customer retention and company revenue

Can you tell me something about a time you disagreed with your supervisor?

Sounds like a trap to that issue. If interviewers ask this question, they want to find out how you approach the conflict with a superior in particular.

The interviewer is informed of the fact that there is conflict, so the interviewer doesn't try to provoke your frustration, the interviewer only wants to know how you express your differences with a superior.

Interviewers are doing this also to learn how well you are going to work with a boss and your ability to make compromises.

Playing the victim

When you answer that question you're going to focus on:

How the dispute with your boss has made you learn how to deal with colleagues better

mention the skill and ability that helped you handle the situation

Explain the situation that led to the disagreement (be brief)

You should also avoid:

It is too long to disagree

Be disrespectful when talking about your supervisor

Sample answer

"I disagreed with my boss about making sales representatives and customer care executives work during the weekends in my role as a human resources manager. Instead of talking to her were the executives in sales and customer service were I talked privately in her office about it. I've been open and honest with her about how I believe these people feel they're being overused. After our conversation, the reason for the decision was apparent to me.

The decision was made because we have a huge customer coming out even more than weekdays during the weekends and we can't afford to lose it. The team is working on a compensation plan, she also explained to me. It occurred to me then that the dispute was a pure misunderstanding. The dispute made me understand the value of communication and how problems can be better addressed at their formative stage.

OPINION BASED INTERVIEW QUESTIONS AND ANSWERS

The opinion-based interview question might be a bit confusing to plan for because it is a combination of both the standard interview question and the interview question about conduct. Just as the name sounds, sometimes the opinion-based interview question seeks to know your stands about a particular issue in the workplace or your field of work.

Many opinion-based interview questions you'd possibly be asked would include how to respond in a given situation.

What would you do if you had a boss?

The question could be a little tricky. Interviewers are asking this question because they want to find out how well you can deal with someone who has a different philosophy than you and how well you can handle and interact with people.

If you answer that question you will focus on the following:

How to handle the situation

Speak about your response to that situation

Chat about what you'll be doing

don't do the following:

Don't dwell on the negative area of the whole

Don't make wrong decisions

Sample answer

"If I've got a bad boss I'd try to understand the person's personality and know what the problem is or what's making the manager unpleasant. If the boss becomes violent then I'd try to understand what's likely to make the boss upset and try not to do so. I'd look for what makes the boss happy then, and do it more often.

Finally, I'm going to try my best to understand why the boss acts like that and look for a better way of behaving towards the guy.

I'm always going to ask other staff how they treated the boss over time.

What kind of supervision do you want to work with?

Employers frequently ask this question to clarify how you would function under observation, or have an idea. They ask this question to discover out how well you'd fit into their style of administration.

We most often ask this question to find out about your past experiences with your boss and consider your preference when it comes to the style of management.

When answering this question you concentrate on the following:

The attributes of the work you like most

State how to respond to the various management styles

Think through your answers before you attempting

You should also stay away from the following:

Don't criticize a past supervisor

Do not get carried away with your answer, and know where to draw the line

Sample answers

"my ideal boss would be one who facilitates good communication between himself and the members of the team. I think communication is a key factor in working together as a successful team and even one that can move the whole company forward."

"I'd like to work with a manager who'll give me a reason for doing more. When I was working as a salesman, I used to work with a supervisor who always argues and yells that our sales can be higher, no matter how much work they do. Before she leaves she was replaced by another boss, the new supervisor was always noticing the little we have done and encouraging us to do more. Working with the new supervisor increased the effortless turnaround. This is the kind of boss I'd like to work for.'

how can you define a good work environment?

Employers recognize that workers in an atmosphere in which they want to be, are happier and more productive. An atmosphere that better suits their style of personality. Interviewees will typically ask you this question to see if they already have you in the work environment.

Before replying to the issue, concentrate on the following:

Research the organization to find out about the structure of the company and know whether it is a large or small enterprise, have an idea of work/life balance, company size, etc.

Speaking about a climate which will make growth and development easier

Insist on your belief in operating in a team-oriented environment

Talk about how you'd rather work, be careful that's in line with the vision of the company

You should also stay away from the following:

Avoid talking about a place of work that allows for several vacations, flexible working hours, and fun.

Avoid building your reaction around people

Stop fusing the company into your response

Sample answers

"my ideal working environment is one that is based around working as a team, one that allows team members to work together to achieve success by taking advantage of their various skills and abilities, while at the same time growing the potential of everyone. While I was studying your business, I found that you were paying a great deal of attention to promoting collaboration. That has inspired me about the job. I find out I work better in an atmosphere that is inspiring and positive.

"I love working in a small environment, with few people. This doesn't mean I can't succeed in a large and well-organized organization. I worked for coca-cola, a huge organization, but I enjoy being part of a success story that's why I'd like to work in a small company rather than a big one.

I find the subject-matter more fascinating than others. I see approaches coming up that grow a trilling company rather than following the formulas laid down. I read carefully the meaning of this position and found that it was all in order.

what do you describe as a satisfying job?

To know what you are passionate about in your career, what kind of job can offer happiness, interviewers ask these questions, they want to know what your definition of a job is. The interviewees often ask this question to learn how you will be happy with their work.

You will focus on the following when answering this question:

Focus on an area of your work which is related to the role you apply for

Concentrate on being positive when thinking about your work environment

You should focus on other issues such as growth and development etc.

You should stop the following, too:

You should not concentrate on aspects of the job this is very small

Do not give a rehearsed response which has nothing to do with the job

Sample answers

"I would characterize my ideal job as one that will encourage me to use my skills and abilities in the best way. One that is constantly encouraging me to put more effort into doing more. I look forward to a career that will give me room for growth and good control, which are the things I have found in this job.

Generally speaking, a productive working environment full of people who want to do more will inspire me to do my best.

"My ideal job is one that will include me working alone and collaborating with others to deliver great results. I am inspired by myself because I want to push myself beyond the mark. My ideal job would be one that would allow me to work with like minds to achieve the goal set and make use of my abilities. I am also interested in working in a position that will give me the chance to add value to the company's growth and a place that will encourage my growth and development.'

What does motivation mean to you?

The problem is every growing and can easily be misinterpreted as well. So, you should be vigilant about your responses when you're asked this question. Make sure your answers are correct enough and also try to tie your responses to the job you are applying for.

When you are answering this question, you should focus on:

Talking about a real thing that motivates you

Work on tying up anything that motivates you to the job you are applying for

Always give useful instances that would help make your point clearer

you should also avoid:

Do not say the important things are things that inspire you

Don't lie

Sample answers

"it's one thing that motivates me to set targets and hit them. I'm an outcome-oriented person, and realizing that I wanted to do something and finally accomplished it at the right time and also with a great result is one thing that will always drive me to do more" "learning new things motivates me and gives me a reason to keep going.

Problem-solving is one of my highest skills and I love challenges. Challenges force me into doing more while I am learning. I feel that learning never stops to beat the competition, especially in a competitive world like ours, one should always submit oneself to learning. One thing that will always inspire me to do a job, is the fact that I can learn something new. Looking at the job description, I know it's going to be a motivational job for me.

How can you describe success in your job?

As straightforward as this question may be, when you answer this question it is also crucial that you pay maximum attention. When administrators ask this question, they want to understand your work ethics and your personality. They also want to understand your measuring system as much as the interviewer wants to understand the work ethic.

Many interviewers want to know how to assess progress if you get the job, or whether you've got some strategy at all.

Make sure you do, when answering this question:

You give examples of times you have achieved success in fulfilling your mission

Explain the steps you have taken to get your interviewer successful

You can also think about the goals you set for yourself, and how you were able to exceed the goal's expectation.

Be honest

You should avoid the following:

You should avoid talking about successes that aren't actual or that are not business-related.

Avoid boasting

Avoid exaggeration

 avoid sounding very perfect, it will not give you room for improvement

Sample answers

"I define success as not only doing the best in my job but my team's as well. I think going beyond the expectations set for me and those set for the team is what I find to be a success. If the team can achieve goals both individually and collectively, that's a win for me.

" for me, accomplishment is more than expected in doing my work and knowing that what I do brings real value to the organization. Just as my work adds value to my life and other people's lives.

How do you describe your dream company?

Do not rush to spill out that dream of working in a business that will be able to pay you six figures, exposure to expensive holidays, flexible working hours when interviewers ask you this question. It's not all those that the interviewer wants to hear. The interviewer needs something to hear that will persuade him you're the right person for the job.

If you want to ask this question you should take note of the following:

Be serious about what is an ideal place to work for you

Ensure that your dream conforms with that of the company

Pay close attention to what you can offer the company too

You should stop the following, too:

You should stop exaggeration and avoid saying this is the best job if not

Avoid using a single employer as an example which may be risky

Sample answers

"for me, my dream business is one that will help me better leverage my skills and abilities to contribute to the company's overall success. I respect a firm that respects and appreciates outstanding performance."

"my dream business is one where I will contribute to the company's success. A place I will get new opportunities that will help me make better use of my skills. It would also be a perfect company to give me the ability to develop my career."

what is your definition of failure?

Counting achievements is fine, but interviewees often think it is important that they know what you call failure. Interviewees ask this question because they aspire to understand what failure to see if it aligns with the expectations set for that particular position implies to you.

Take note of the following when you want to answer this question:

Make sure what you find to be a failure is in line with what the company considers as a failure for that role or in general

Just be honest and straight forward

You should also stay away from the following:

You should not lie

Speak too much so as not to build unrealistic expectations for yourself

Sample answer

"for me, I define failure as the incapability of someone to satisfy a job requirement. Failing isn't all about not working hard to get things done, it's about not being able to deliver a result that will validate the work you've done."

"I describe failure as a situation where, over time, someone has not been able to contribute to the company's overall success.

how do you set your job goals?

This question can be answerable very easily as it is straight forward. Interviewers sometimes ask this question because they want to know how structured you are, and they also want to know how you set your goals, or whether you have any goals at all.

When answering this question, you should concentrate on:

Your practical approach to establishing your professional goals.

An indication as to why you define your business goals

You should also avoid the following

Do not be specific in your answer to the question

Sample answer

"I set my job targets by carefully examining my tasks for both short and long-term tasks, knowing what the result of those tasks is anticipated and how I plan to perform the task. Once I begin to perform all the tasks for a given day, I look at the task according to their level of importance. I start with a smaller job with a tiny target so there's room for progress. I set my job goals essentially with the desired outcome in mind."

How do you deal with deadlines on multiple tasks?

This is a very tricky problem that can cause you to lose your balance unless you are careful. Employers mostly ask this question because they want to understand how you are going to meet the deadlines that can come up during the job.

When answering this question, you should take note of the following:

Always try to guide the interviewer through your plans to meet deadlines in the job or overall the mission

Display that you are well organized and give good priority

Avoid doing the following:

Complaining about deadlines and how you have to do too many things at once

Don't give the impression you're lazy

Sample answers

"regardless of what the task is, I set out to see the best way to proceed. I would organize the organization of the most important task to the least importance. They would also ask for help if needed."

"First, I would maintain a positive mood regardless of the scale of this operation, and then develop a plan that would help me get results considering the term. The term, I would like to extend extensively."

MAKING A PRESENTATION

Giving a presentation

Sometimes you will be asked to make a presentation during the interview. This will not normally be given to you. The employer will explain what is required when receiving the invitation to your interview. If you are unsure, do not hesitate to contact your employer for more information. Presentations are increasingly part of the interview because public speaking is involved in many tasks. Some jobs often involve talking to groups of people. Some examples of this type of work are public relations assistants, training agents, or marketing managers. Many other jobs will require occasional presentations to team members, outside visitors, or colleagues. Also, any administrative or supervisory work will often involve talking to staff groups and an employer may use a presentation to assess their confidence when standing in front of a group to see how they behave. Employers will be interested to see how much they can lead and lead a group and provide opportunities for group participation, if applicable.

Another reason for candidates to make a presentation, even if it is not an important part of the job, is that it allows each candidate to provide a lot of information to the interviewer. A five- or ten-minute presentation explaining why you think you are the best candidate for the position will replace the need for half an hour of questions on the same topic. This implies that you have the opportunity to present your arguments as you see fit. You can decide on the best way to present yourself to the potential employer. From an employer's perspective, this means that candidates can be compared by talking about the same general issues in each presentation and the interview itself can be used for more detailed questions.

Some interviews may require you to make a presentation without prior information. In this case, it usually takes some time to prepare just before making the presentation. This will be to test how much you can think of on your feet, select and present material in the short term and keep your freshness under pressure.

Planning your presentation

You are being asked to give a presentation to explore how well you can:

Present with clarity;

Concisely arrange material;

Plan your ideas logically;

Explain key points;

Have an impact on an audience.

You have to plan and repeat a good presentation to do it confidently. Make no mistake in thinking that you can speak quietly without at least as much preparation as you give your answers to the interview questions that may arise. Even if you are talking about something you know well, there is time to gather your ideas clearly and logically. Under the pressure of time and sensation.

Nervous during the day, it is wonderful to see how, if you are not well prepared, your mind may become empty and you may find it overwhelming.

Then you can spend enough time thinking about the title you have been given to prepare for the day. Even if you haven't been given the topic before, you don't need to panic. You will usually set aside a preparation time throughout the day, often up to an hour, to gather your thoughts and ideas to present to the interview panel. The subject is rarely completely unexpected. He is probably concerned about some aspects of the work and that time spent thinking about and planning possible topics for the presentation will be well spent.

Types of presentation

Here are 10 examples of different presentation topics that could be defined. These presentation topics vary depending on the position required. However, in any case, you need to think about what you want to highlight as the main key points:

1. Prepare a five-minute summary of your ideas for developing this post.

2. Prepare a 15-minute presentation on one of your priorities for this role.

3. We want you to talk for 10 minutes about the main issues that you think you have with this organization.

4. Prepare a 10-minute overview of your main achievements to date.

5. Say in five minutes or less why we should give you this post.

6. Explain in 15 minutes how you see the main strengths, weaknesses, opportunities, and threats to this company.

7. Talk about a case in which you have managed the change.

8. We want to move to a more customer-centric culture. What advice would you give us?

9. What would you recommend to help survive this economic downturn?

10. Tell us in 20 minutes how you can get ahead in this department.

Sometimes you will be asked to submit several types of documents. The exercises can be defined where you need to evaluate the material and then present your decisions to the panel, both in writing and in person.

The exercises may include simulated aspects of the work for which you are applying, for example, a work exercise for a higher administrative position. Here, you may be required to read as many documents as they would in a container waiting for your opinions, decisions, and actions. A letter can lead to a problem that has come out among staff members; another email may cover the need for a group meeting on a strategic issue where you need to take the initiative to set the agenda, and another document may ask for your advice on a technical issue. You will be judged on your capability to prioritize, make decisions, and handle different situations depending on how you process and respond to the documents in this simulation. Knowing the organization in question and feeling clear about the priorities that exist will help us to tackle this type of activity. For example, in a common exercise like the one described above, think about which element will give priority.

Another type of presentation is involved in a discussion. Discussions are often used for jobs or courses that involve a high level of human skills. They may come out with other candidates, sometimes with other staff members, sometimes together. An illustration of this type of approach is that of some appointments for the higher civil service in which candidates are asked to advise on a current issue to a person who acts as a government minister in the department in which they will work.

Topics can be given for discussion under observation and will often be evaluated based on your ability to work with the group rather than how their own opinions are expressed. This means that it would be most important to help others participate and encourage an open and comprehensive debate that wins all the arguments. If you can handle this kind of activity, you must first think of your tactics. For example, in a sales environment, your ability to `` connect " with others, adapt your conversation to theirs, and reach a mutual agreement can be impressive, while for the work of a political researcher, in-depth analysis and detailed and firm conclusions can indicate success.

Prepare a presentation

You can prepare to give an even more comprehensive presentation than you would for a simple interview. Take some time to think through the question first if you have solved it before: discuss it with others, write notes and think about it. If you do not have the subject and will not be provided until the day of the interview, you can always make valuable preparation. What kind of question might be asked? This could be an example, are there particular aspects of the job you want to hear? Is the organization now going through some kind of change or challenge? What do you think are the most significant parts of the job and how do you manage it? You should be prepared to talk about one of these points during the day.

After getting some initial ideas, try to structure your session into three key points for easy follow-up. Don't try to order too much information, since some key points are better than some confusing documents.

Here is an example of planning for a presentation on topic number 4 'your main work achievements to date'; you might decide to have as your three key points:

My main achievements at work;

My specific role in these achievements;

What characteristics I demonstrated.

Rehearsing your presentation

No actor takes the stage without the proper procedures, the last in full dress. We must do the same. Exercise what you want to say by voice to get the key point.

Practice in front of a mirror, so you know how you are going to looks;

Friends, so they can verify that what you are saying makes sense;

Watch, so you can make the time of your presentation precisely. You must respect the time limit set for you. Researchers often interrupt him if he is overwhelmed, which could completely ruin his presentation. Too many presentations are too long, make sure yours is not one of them.

Projecting yourself

Making a presentation requires a little more energy than normal maintenance because it goes for performance. Always present your presentation standing up if you have the opportunity. It is easier for people to focus on what they say and if they are seen clearly. You have to present your material in a slightly larger size than the real thing with bigger gestures, more projection and variety in your voice, and more animation than you would normally. If you think that your nerves might prevent you from playing this way, you should consider it as a show for the public. You will mainly be asked to make a presentation if the position in question means that you often occupy that position. Think about how you could do group presentations if you did the work and that might help you today: you can imagine at work.

Use visual aid

We can offer easy computers, flipcharts, or other visual aids to use in your presentation. Think carefully before using a program such as Microsoft powerpoint to provide a series of screens to accompany your presentation. Unless you are dealing with a large audience or need to distribute complex material, it will normally not be beneficial for you to use this type of presentation software. In a short presentation, a simple copy of your main points will be enough visual support to improve your presentation and PowerPoint can also be useful to produce.

Don't try to use something you're not sure or comfortable with. When you are stressed, this is the best time to experiment with unknown equipment or technology. In addition to the technical difficulties, you must resist the temptation to reproduce everything you say in PowerPoint or wake up your hearing. Every visual backup you need to use should add interest to what it says and reinforce your key points. Use as many images as possible instead of words and avoid numbers and statistics. Tables and graphs, if clearly illustrated, can be

Way to pass on complex information. There are fantastic amounts of prints available, including pictures, maps, and symbols. See clip art on your computer: royalty-free images that you can use as you wish in any presentation. Don't be tempted to be overly ambitious - keep your graphics simple so they add to your presentation, not hurt you. Talk your message, not technology.

You have to wonder: what is this presentation? How does the use of presentation software contribute to my impact? If you are presenting to a big group, it may be useful to use software to demonstrate where you went with your presentation. Powerpoint can also be useful if you need to visually show a complicated relationship, such as an economic downturn. A graph can highlight the facts much simpler than listening to detailed statistics searches.

A senior government employee who conducts frequent interviews told me:

"I always ask for presentations and I'm afraid of people coming in to insert the laptop. It's necessarily a tedious presentation where everything they show me, they've already told me. All I want to know is that they can stand up and make a sensible presentation; I don't want to see endless and useless graphics on a screen that duplicate everything and add nothing. If you can't attractively talk to me without help, then using PowerPoint will certainly not help you at work. "

What to do and how to not

Keep it simple and direct.

Summarize your presentation into a document or checklist to keep the panel (make sure your name is. Take advantage of the presentation when you're done, to showcase yourself as that part of the job.

Don't throw them too much; you can go beyond the heads of all present.

Do not speak in a language that is not normal; avoid slang and initials.

Don't try to gather too much information in one brief presentation; less is more

Points to remember

A good presentation does not happen by accident, they must work.

The impression you want employers to have is that you are the highest bidder and full of great ideas.

The key structure of your presentation will help the audience understand.

Try to include a visual element to convey your points.

The delivery of your presentation needs as much work as the content. Practice makes perfect.

HOW TO OVERCOME FEAR FOR INTERVIEWS

How to overcome a fear of interviews

If your hands are swinging and your knees turn to jelly every time you enter a job interview, you're not alone. However, you should not be afraid of interviewing to limit your career prospects. The first step to overcoming your fear to clear your mind regarding the interview. After that, spend a lot of time and effort on preparation, so that you feel more confident in day d. Finally, learn some strategies for conducting the interview.

Interview preparation

1. Familiarize yourself with the position you require. Learn as many as you can about the job you are looking for, the people who will interview you, and the company itself. Read the company's website and find the profiles of its researchers on LinkedIn. The more information you find, the more secure you will feel during the interview.

If you don't do the work in advance, the researchers may be able to tell you that you haven't prepared much and that it might take you less seriously.

Also, make sure you take the time to think about how this job fits your career goals and how you express yourself during the interview.

2. Save your cv. Extend your resume from one place to another so you can talk about your past work experience without leaving it blank. Consider if you want to highlight any of your particular works and, if so, what they mean.

For instance, you may want to talk about how a previous job gives you important skills that you will need to succeed in that job.

Find examples that demonstrate your skills and write some summaries. For case, If the interviewer asks you to focus more on your programming skills, you should be able to list your skills and provide examples of how you used them, such as when you built a new one. Interface to a large company database.

3. Think about how I will answer the most common interview questions. Some questions tend to arise during each interview. Find a list of these frequently asked questions and think about how you want to answer them.

Answer the questions honestly, but do not look bad in the process.

For example, if the interviewer asks you why you want this job, don't just say "I need the money," even if it's true. Say something specific at work, such as "I find it satisfying to keep things organized and help people find what they need."

4. Remember that it doesn't matter if you don't know all the answers. It is perfectly acceptable to leave the interviewer who does not know the answer to a question. You can always come back to them with an answer later. Admitting that you do not know the answer to something and returning to the interviewer with an answer later, shows that if you do not have an answer, you will find it. He even shows that he traces the things he says he will do.

Try saying something like "I don't always have an answer, but I will think." it also gives you a reason to send a follow-up note or email to the interviewer after the interview.

5. Ask a friend to train. Send someone to do an interview simulation with you, to practice answering real-time questions. Give your colleague a list of questions you aspire to practice answering, but also ask some unexpected questions.

Invite your friend to share your thoughts on how they talk and behave, and how to answer questions.

You can also enhance your interview skills by filming yourself. Looking from the outside will give you a good idea of what you need to improve.

Pay attention to your nonverbal communication, such as your body language, voice, or facial expressions. Think about what your caller's going to say about that stuff.

6Think of a few questions that you want the interviewer to pose. If you ask your question during the interview you will make a good impression. Plugin your questions ahead of time.

Make sure you search before asking questions. Do not ask if the answer is easy to find.

Good questions include: "why do you like working here?", "what are the main goals of the business?" and "how do you assess the success of an employee in this business?"

Changing your mindset

1. Change your perspective. A job interview is just a conversation, not an interrogation. Its purpose is to see if you are a good candidate for the company (and vice versa). While it is important to give the best impression possible, the interviewer does not analyze each of his movements for error, therefore, he tries to relax and focus on the true purpose of the interview.

2. Also remember that you are interviewing your employer as well. An interview is a two-way street. Yes, employers have the power to decide whether or not to employ them, Yet interviews do allow them to see if they want to work for a company or not. Take an active attitude towards your interviews and throughout the process, you'll feel more confident.

3. Focus on your strengths. Think of everything that makes you an excellent employee: your education, your experience, and your personal qualities. Remember, if a potential employer calls you for an interview, you've already noted these good qualities, then start with a positive impression of yourself.

You do not need to have years of experience or extensive training to be a good employee. Personal qualities such as persistence, organization, and excellent interpersonal skills can also make you a serious candidate for a job.

Consider how your weaknesses can become strengths. For example, if you tend to accept too many projects simultaneously, you may learn to practice planning and prioritizing intentions.

4. He knows that rejection is not the end of the world. It's not fun to give a bad interview or pretend to be a job, but it happens to everyone. Don't be too harsh on yourself when an interview is not going well. Instead, think about what you can acquire from the experience and remember that there are many other jobs.

For example, if your mind goes blank in the middle of an interview, you may want to spend more time rehearsing before the next one.

Getting through interviews

1. Get there first. Give yourself sufficient time to get an interview. Leave home as needed so that traffic delays or bad weather will not delay them. Once there, take a few minutes to compose yourself. It is good to look several minutes early, but do not enter the building more than five or ten minutes in advance. Wait outside or in the car until almost time for maintenance.

If you're waiting in a reception area, make sure that you're a professional.

Sometimes the interviewer asks the receptionist how he behaves while waiting.

2. Take a deep breath. Take a deep breath to calm down and relax before and during the interview. If you feel tense, breathe slowly and slowly through your nose.

Breathe in your abdomen, not in your chest.

3. Use safe body language. Even if you are not certain, you can "lend" some confidence with your body language. Stand or sit upright, shoulders. Maintain good eye contact with the interviewer throughout the interview and do not forget to smile.

When you act like a confident person, you start to feel more confident.

4. Be yourself. Make no mistake about putting your best foot forward for false personality. If you are confident, your true personality will eventually come out anyway, so be honest. Speak and present as you normally would.

5. Be honest if you are nervous. If fear invades you, say so. Being honest will help you relax a bit. Probably the researcher will not judge you negatively; being nervous shows that you are worried about getting the job.

For example, if your mind goes wild on a subject, say something like "I'm sorry, I'm a little nervous now." then he takes a deep breath and tries the question again.

REASONS FOR FAILURE A LABOR INTERVIEW

Failure to get a real shot of confidence in a job interview and trust is everything in this game. Recovering from a bad experience can be very difficult so what's the answer? Make sure you make no of the following mistakes which are the most common reasons for a failed job interview.

Reasons To Fail A Job Interview

1. Bad preparation

Bad preparation is an obvious killer and 75% of interviews fail because the candidate didn't expect some of the questions asked ... I think everyone agrees that a person without preparation is easily discernible in every situation ...

So here is the fact and applies throughout the world: Employers have done the work to find you, so expect you to do your homework too! Given the number of requests you receive, you may want to consider yourself lucky to get an interview and should take advantage of this opportunity to prepare properly.

What do you need to do?

When you have a scheduled interview, you should not only prepare but also find a way to practice and perform with someone. You should come to the interview with an idea of what they might ask ... and what you shouldn't ask.

To give you the smallest chance of doing a job interview, it is best to repeat with an appropriate professional coach who will do auto marketing techniques and comments to distinguish and make a good impression.

2. displaying a negative attitude.

Showing a negative attitude is another way to avoid a second interview and reduce the chances of getting a job, one of the 5 main reasons for failing in a job interview.

You're going to complain and criticize everything ... If you say bad things about your former boss or company ... If you are defensive, evasive, or brutal ... well, you can also cancel this interview!

My best advice is to stay positive at all times. Before you criticize, remember: you're not perfect ... in fact, nobody is, but giving the impression that you think you're perfect is a surefire way to do it in a job interview. and then:

Do not criticize just to establish differences in opinions, cultures, practices, or processes.

Do not defend and justify; just explain

It's enough to say, "I don't know, but I'll find him..."

He doesn't seem insulted or ashamed; smile and use your charm to ease the atmosphere...

Don't take things personally; you don't know this person...

3. Lack of enthusiasm.

Lack of enthusiasm can be immediately detected through your body language, your eye contact, and the tone of your voice ... In fact, your hand can say everything ...

Tell yourself, "Why do I go to this interview?" If the answer is "I don't go to this interview?" ... Then, read the job description in detail, visit their website and consult Glassdoor for company reviews; If you have always believed that this job is not what you want, you can do two things:

Number 1: You can use this quote to practice your interview skills in a live scene.

Number 2: You can use this Network Meeting. Even if you're not chosen for a specific role, you can still talk to your LinkedIn interviewer, thank them for the interview and "follow" their route to LinkedIn. Many of my clients consider their job in contact with people that they met during an interview.

Now, do you want this job?

So be sure to prove it! Employers expect nothing short of passion! If you can't convince employers you're going to be so enthusiastic about this, don't rely too much on your long-term commitment and longevity.

4. vague and dishonest answers

Wave and Dishonest are common practices in an interview situation, and employers have known it.

Employers can see through invented and dishonest responses. Then, of course, keep the conversation positive and constructive and do not interfere in past failures or negative circumstances. Just follow these rules and it will be difficult to do in a job interview:

For every failure, what was your learning?

For any weaknesses, what is your remedy or solution?

Always have it in mind that the problem is not the problem, but how you solved it ...

5. Lack of clarity

Lack of clarity is not only exhaustive for an interviewer, but it is also frustrating and irritating.

If you're not sure what brings you to the table for a particular job, chances are you'll never be successful in this role.

So what do we have to do?

Ask yourself "who can contribute to this job?" and make a list of all the assets you have: professional, personal, and polite ...

Many people fail in a job interview because they don't do their research. Read the job description in detail, list all the requirements, and explain how to meet them.

CONCLUSION

The secret to answering job interview questions is just a matter of understanding the process. Researchers are essentially looking for evidence that the people they interview have the skills and experience. All you need to do is to provide the proof to make sure that you are protected before your competition.

The first thing to do next to answer the interview questions, before the interview itself, is to know everything you can about the job. Read the job description, if available, to make sure you understand the role in the organization and what specific commitments are involved. In particular, you need to think about how it can be demonstrated that you have the skills and experience to work. Remember that the skills, knowledge, and experiences you have accumulated can be transferred to a variety of situations. For example, consider work as part of a team. You may have experience working in a team that is very different from the position you require but still works in a team. Therefore, the problems of teamwork are the same.

In the interview itself, to respond effectively to interview questions, you must talk about real and practical examples of your work and your experiences. For example, when asked how you can handle a particular situation, do not try to talk about hypothetical situations. Instead, you should talk about real-life examples in which you have dealt with similar situations.

You have to be positive and not be afraid to talk about your accomplishments. However, don't leave too much to face and pretend that you have done more than you and that the companies you are about to disappear into without you. Be realistic and talk about your true useful real talent.

The purpose of the interview is to ask the answers to the questions. The best thing you can do before preparing for an interview. That said, you probably have questions that will make you think.

There is also the danger of being over-prepared in the sense that all you want to do is regurgitate the information in your mind. The best way to answer interview questions is to do it correctly.

In other words, take some time before answering the question. Make sure you understand what is behind the question, ie what they mean by the request. If you are not sure, ask them to repeat.

Don't be afraid to ask what they mean by this request. Now, you might be a little worried about looking silly, asking them to repeat the request, or asking them to clarify, but honestly, it's much better than going to a tangent with an answer that isn't exactly relevant to the request.

Remember, that interviews are all questions and answers, so don't worry about doing well by asking what they mean.

Finally, listen carefully to what they ask. Do not be consumed with what you think you are asking, listen first, then the reason for your request will be revealed more easily.